The Umbrella Picker

A Lost Girl's journey to self-identity
and finding her neurological truth

THE
umbrella
PICKER

Jane
McNeice

I dedicate this book to my daughter Laura, a 'Lost Girl' now found, to my mum who remains lost but no longer lost to me, and to my son, I promise you will be found very soon.

To my husband Steven, and youngest son Ben, though you are not lost, you are no less loved with all my heart.

And to 'The Lost Girls'; one day we will find you all...

The author uses a capital A in Autism when diagnosed, a small a when undiagnosed.

"The privilege of a lifetime is to become who you truly are."

Carl Jung

Contents

Prologue

The sheen of the brown paper bags feels smooth for the little fingers that caress them. Residual paper corners remain attached to the dirty grey cotton string hooked to the side of the serving top. Not all umbrella-shaped paper corners remain, some fall and land in and around the floor, dispersing like seedlings hoping to be the next sapling. The irony is not lost. Little pale hands collect the fallen umbrellas until the floor is clear and ready for the new fall. Each week the little Umbrella Picker clears the floor, handing fists full of them to the silver-haired shop owner to dispose of. They are everywhere on the floor; they are too distracting to the three-year-old little girl. They make her uncomfortable, agitated even. The Umbrella Picker finds satisfaction in picking up the little corners of paper left behind each time a paper bag is torn from the string. The customer takes her crisp brown paper bag of yarn and pattern, and 'The Umbrella Picker' leaves after satisfying her overwhelming need to declutter and clean up.

Had it not been for the muted colours glinting within plastic packets, packets showing the perpetual signs of reopening and closing, the smell would have you think you were in a carpenter's workshop rather than a haberdashery and knitting shop. The well-worn wooden serving top had been made shiny through hands that unravelled those plastic packets, putting balls of wool into brown paper bags

for local knitters who would weave wonders with the yarn
– knitting one, purling one – creating a weave of warmth
for the lucky, or unlucky, recipient. I mean, who in their
right mind really wanted an intarsia jumper?!

The wool shop owner's hands were worn from knitting
and packing, with a smile that sparkled and reached her
firm but friendly blue eyes, seeing through Dame Edna
spectacles, and blending with coarse silver shoulder-length
hair. She talked the language of knitters with a younger
customer seeking to understand the 1970s knitting pattern
laid out on the worktop. The cacophony continues for the
Umbrella Picker as she works to satisfy her urge and calm
her active mind.

Had the women in the shop have been aware of what
they had witnessed back then – the connection to my now
diagnosis – the search would have commenced there,
and it would have been led by my mother. But, in 1978,
understanding was not great, and many would wager it still
is not. They instead titled me 'The Umbrella Picker', the
little girl who would come into the shop every Saturday
afternoon with her mummy, and who would clear a weeks'
worth of paper corners from the floor.

Today, my hope is for this book to find its way to other
readers who remain lost, just like I was for a very long time.
These readers may see themselves and their truth within
it. It may reveal to them who they really are, it may 'find'
them.

CHAPTER ONE

The Day I Stopped Searching

"A wise man once observed that if you study an object of nature intently enough, if you focus upon it long enough with all your powers of concentration and attention, there comes a point at which the macrocosm behind the object is suddenly revealed."

Unknown Wise Man, *Neurotribes*
by Steve Silberman (2015)[1]

Most people do not know their last supper. In fact, most people would not *want* to know. The few that do are offered this privilege because they are about to meet their end. I was offered that privilege, not because I was meeting my end, but because an end *was* about to happen. My last supper consisted of chicken, potato dauphinoise and chantenay carrots, followed by white chocolate panna cotta at a hotel in Hemel Hempstead. I had taken the long and worthwhile journey from South Yorkshire to meet a lady who would change my life irrevocably.

On Tuesday 22nd June 2021, I entered the consulting room in Hemel Hempstead to meet a psychotherapist qualified to undertake neurodiversity clinical assessments.

On meeting Deborah, I immediately felt a warmth and kindness supportive of someone who understood *ME*. That was something I had not felt before. This person knew *me*, she knew the type of person I was, and understood my support needs. It felt comforting at a time when I was feeling incredibly nervous. I sat in a chair opposite her desk. We engaged in a little small talk, not easy for me as I struggle with this, though I did happen to say, "I'm really looking forward just to finding out one way or another, I feel like I've waited for *so* long." Deborah held my gaze and replied, "I feel as if I know you already. I've read your blog, your website, and all the documents you have submitted. Everything you have illustrated tells me that you are Autistic. What we will do today is simply work through some questions and expand on the detail a little more." I am Autistic! BOOM! I don't think I even remember the few minutes that happened after that.

One of the most moving things in the world is seeing the light come on in someone's eyes, especially when they've been lost in the dark for so long. Deborah bore witness to my light that morning.

At that precise moment, it was as if a hazmat-suited angel had walked into the consulting room and lifted the weight of my past from my shoulders to remove and detoxify it before gradually returning it to me over the next few weeks. I cried, and for the next two hours tried desperately to stay focused on Deborah's questions, while slipping off into a reverie of 'Wow, I have found *me*. I finally know *who* I am!' The questions were detailed, we unpicked the past and the present, reflecting now in the light of Autism, and at the end of the assessment Deborah reiterated the diagnosis and that she had not disproved her initial clinical judgement based on the extra information. You might be wondering if my GP had referred me to Deborah, but this was not my path to assessment. I had pursued a private Autism assessment because I had waited far too long already, and did not want to be exposed to unnecessary waiting times so often experienced within the statutory services. I had self-identified that I was Autistic, by chance. Deborah merely corroborated what I had already worked out for myself.

Deborah would now draft a report of our session with the information provided, including recommendations for support, and the report would be signed off by a second party, a qualified psychiatrist. I left the consulting room ready to navigate the M1 home and began my reprocessing of everything I had believed to be true.

Twenty-second of June 2021 had solidified something I already knew, something I thought I was well prepared for. What I now know is that I was not nearly as prepared as I had first believed. You see, most people think the end of the journey is getting an accurate diagnosis, but if that diagnosis is Autism, or any life-changing diagnosis, it is in fact the *start* of a journey. A journey of reprocessing and reframing everything you thought to be true about yourself. I had thought I was ready for the final piece of the jigsaw because I had discovered it myself a year earlier, so I'd already had twelve months to roll it around in my brain, get a feel for it, layer it over my life, and contextualise it. But the neurological shift I experienced that day on being told categorically by a qualified Autism Assessor was something else – life changing! The neurological truth had generated the most significant shift in my brain and, without doubt, the most positive clinical outcome of any psychological intervention I have ever received, and it's fair to say I have tried a few over the years!

I called my husband Steven. "I'm Autistic!" I blurted. Steven is a man of few words, but I detected a level of surprise in his breathing and tone. I think Steven, amongst others, did not fully believe that I would be diagnosed Autistic. That said, his stance on the matter has always been that it does not make any difference to him. I am still me. It does not change anything.

I had told a small number of family and friends that I thought I was Autistic. Most of them questioned it, or their faces and eyes told me they were not entirely convinced. I also predict the reason was that they were still thinking, *but you do not look Autistic*. Society seems to want a 'look'. I don't know what that 'look' is, but I have a few Autistically scripted retorts in preparation for those who say it, and there have been a number already.

Our bathroom tiler: "…I'm not being funny, but you don't look Autistic."

"Well, Nick, it must be because I've put my hair up in a different way today," or, "You don't look neurotypical, so that makes two of us who don't look to type," and other antagonistic remarks. I will not use either of these, for reasons I will come to explain, but nevertheless they have entered my psychological scripting catalogue.

I then called my twenty-six-year-old daughter – one of the other most important people in my life – and told her my truth. Laura was one of the few people who already recognised me to be Autistic. Laura's response was, "How do you feel? Are you pleased?" She was pre-empting future emotions that could be her own. I was on a high, with an impending sense that it could not last forever. The high included tears: several tears for every year of suffering I had endured, and several more of joy. To put it into a context that others might relate, I felt like a lottery winner, or someone who had just been told they were no longer diseased, or terminal. The emotional outbursts occurred all the way home, and several times over the next few weeks. They still happen now, sometimes in the middle of the night when I wake in disbelief that it has all happened and the tears start to flow.

Over the next few days, I shared my neurological truth with those close to me. There are still some who have yet to comment on my diagnosis. I think many people just don't know what to say. They do not know whether to commiserate you as if you have cancer, or to congratulate you. The latter is my preference; the diagnosis is for me a phenomenally good thing, not a bad thing.

My mum was someone who found it difficult to believe and comprehend. She blamed herself for not having noticed the signs in me as a child because she too knew the suffering I had endured. Her response was, "But you could hold a full adult conversation by the time you were

✗ Letter to my mom about autism
✗ Letter to my mom

5

eighteen months old, so we wouldn't have thought it in a million years." Very much one of the traits, I think. I had a precocious vocabulary from an early age. Mum's frame of reference was in fact her own blind spot in this instance. Like many, she was linking Autism with learning disability. This was understandable, since my late brother Robert had been diagnosed Autistic with a learning disability by the time he was eight years old. The greatest focus had been placed on Robert's more apparent needs, his learning disability in particular, with much less said about the Autism. I suspect this was because it was the easier part for my parents to understand. Having a learning disability also meant that Robert would likely be identified young. Close family members had noticed signs early. Our maternal grandparents had another similar age grandchild, our cousin Karen, and had quickly spotted the stark difference in early development between the two children. My cousin Karen and I remain very close today, we have a sisterly relationship and text one another near daily, looooooong texts, so long that we define them by how many swipes it takes to read them. Karen is one of my life supports and confidantes, we share so much via the written word. I do hope I am this to Karen also. If you are reading this 'r' Karen, this one is more than a few swipes! Never mind the cuppa, you had better fill the teapot and take a seat…

Mum was resistant to the idea that Robert had developmental difficulties, as any parent might initially be. It is not the dream you have when you think, *let's have a baby, let's become parents*. The dream we all have is a fit healthy child, mentally and physically able. Such dreams can be thwarted catastrophically. Once mum had accepted Robert's identity and challenges, she fought like any lioness would for her cub. She wanted support and waged that campaign throughout Robert's life, and to his final moments. At age eight, Robert was transferred to a specialist school in Rossington near Doncaster, a school for children with special educational needs. Many of the children had physical and mental disabilities, and some required high levels of support. Robert grew up to be a person who embraced disability. He did not fear it like so many still do, he was not uncomfortable by it. This was one of the many attributes in Robert that I refer to as his 'sparkle'.

Robert had to catch a school bus set up specifically to collect and return the children across Doncaster who attended Rossington Hall. I had been instructed not to share with friends the fact that Robert was attending a 'special school'. A product of their time, and *of* the time, disability was still something that my parents were aware others would shame, and the less others knew the better as far as my parents were concerned. Many of my school friends thought that I was an 'only' child, as I rarely discussed that I had a brother. Robert's disability was at the time another reason for me not to 'fit in' or to belong, so I just kept quiet about it. By the age of six I had internalised ideas that having a disability was bad and viewed as a weakness for others to latch on to for mockery. Guilty by association, I would be on the receiving end of the latter. The saddest thing is that, even today, we are yet to change negative views in the minds of so many. I still see societal prejudice and stigma.

So, I had finally found ME. Me turned out to be Autistic, something that many people still do not fully understand. Autism is a neurological condition. It is a type of neurodiversity. It is not a mental health problem, and it is not episodic, it is permanent. This means that there is no cure for my condition, and for the most part, I would not want to cure it. It is who I am. It is not a disability it is a *difference*; society's lack of understanding and support is what disables Autistic people. Around 1-2% of the population are diagnosed Autistic[2], so we are what I personally describe as a 'minority-minority', exacerbated further by the fact that there is a considerable proportion of people who are autistic but don't even know it, just like I did not until twelve months earlier. When we consider other minority groups in society, for example black and minority ethnic groups, or the LGBTQIA+ community, people in these groups often (but not always) learn early on the minority group to which they identify, much more quickly than an undiagnosed Autistic person might. If you are black, you know you are black once you reach a cognitive level where you are no longer colour-blind, you recognise you are a person of colour and identify as a person of colour, or black, depending on your choice description. If you are gay, you know you are gay once you recognise you prefer the same sex. Yes, you may hide this because of societal stigma and prejudice, but you still know *who* you are from the inside. An undiagnosed Autistic person may recognise, just as I did, that they do not 'fit in' or belong to the majority in society, or what is regarded as 'normal' society, but they do not know why, primarily because they do not know *who* they are. I often hear people say, "But what is 'normal'?" I generally find that comment comes from those who consider themselves somewhere within the realms of 'normal' and are trying to be inclusive by highlighting there is a lot of difference and all is acceptable. But ask anyone who sits on the fringes of society looking in, and they will tell you exactly what 'normal' is. It's one of those things that is unwritten, yet present in everyone's psyche, and illustrates itself through the lines of exclusion. As a societal outsider, I am acutely aware that I am not 'normal'. As someone who for a long time did not know *who* I was, I couldn't identify with anyone, I just knew I did not belong. Knowing *who* you are cannot be overrated and is often underestimated by the 'normal'. I see this in the comments made by clinicians and professionals: "But what difference will a diagnosis make? A diagnosis won't necessarily change anything." It often comes from those who are included, not excluded. They don't understand just how much of a difference it can make and how much it does for so many. The diagnosis *is* an intervention.

Take, for example, self-awareness. It is a vital factor within resilience. Resilience reduces our statistical likelihood of developing a mental health problem. If you do not know *who* you are then you cannot build the necessary self-awareness and self-worth to achieve higher levels of resilience. We can increase our resilience, but we are much better able to if we know *who* we are. So, why is resilience important? It is important because higher levels of resilience helps to prevent stress and, by preventing stress, we can reduce the likelihood of developing a mental and/or physical health problem. Resilience is what we would describe as a protective factor, which is why it reduces our statistical likelihood of developing a mental health problem. So not knowing who I was is the very reason I have always experienced low levels of self-esteem and self-worth. I have not valued myself despite how hard I have tried to be someone of value. My journey of building self-esteem and self-worth began only this year on 22nd of June 2021. At the point of writing, I can already recognise a measured increase in this. I am a little more assertive and outspoken, and things I would have let go previously I am now less likely to. I have also started to accommodate my Autistic needs rather than doing things because I think neurotypicals expect or want me to. Last week, for the first time ever, I asked for help specifically to meet my Autistic needs. I approached the licensor of one of the training products my company offers to ask for support to help me learn a new product. I explained my challenges and requested the option to co-deliver the training course to familiarise myself better with it. I am pleased to say it was granted. This will not be the last time I do this.

Clinically, my diagnosis means I have satisfied the criteria for Autistic Spectrum Disorder under DSM-V (*Diagnostical & Statistical Manual*, 2013), which is:

'Persistent difficulties with social communication and social interaction' and 'restricted and repetitive patterns of behaviours, activities or interests (this includes sensory behaviour), present since early childhood, to the extent that these 'limit and impair everyday functioning'[3]

Though many people are diagnosed as having Asperger Syndrome, this diagnosis has now been removed from the DSM criteria and is no longer ascribed. It is also important to say that some people diagnosed with Asperger's have dissociated from the label following more recent references to Hans Asperger's alleged links with Nazi genocide.

Following suit, the World Health Organisation's 'International Classification of Diseases' has also removed Asperger from Volume 11, which came into effect from 1st January 2022. Reasons apparently include inconsistent application, and some similarities with other spectrum conditions, so I will never know if I would actually have been a so-called 'Aspie', the self-titled name of many of those previously diagnosed with Asperger Syndrome. I am an 'Autie' instead, and a proud one at that. Whilst the World Health Organisation's 'International Classification of Diseases' is the most commonly used diagnostic tool in the UK, used for diagnosing mental health and other neurological conditions, my assessment used DSM-V, which is produced by the APA (American Psychiatric Association), and also well used.

Th DSM-V description above relates to the triad of impairment that Autistic people experience. These are:

- Impaired social communication.
- Impaired social interaction.
- Lack of social imagination.

The eminent Dr Lorna Wing, pioneer in the field of childhood developmental disorders, describes Autistic difficulties as: "Social, social, social, it's *all* social."[4] This reflects the DSM criteria and all Autistic challenges come back to these three elements. For me personally, I fully agree it is the social challenges that are the primary difficulty, and from where all other difficulties originate.

The word Autism itself comes from the Greek 'autos' meaning 'self'. This does not mean Autistic people are selfish, though I have witnessed occasions where others may misinterpret Autistic needs as selfish. It instead relates to the fact that Autistic people are often unable to socially interact and become self-isolated, by choice, or by exclusion. We also spend a great deal of time self-analysing, ever more so if we are undiagnosed and searching for who we are.

As a female, my likelihood of ever being found and receiving a diagnosis of Autism was low, or at the very least low in comparison to my male counterparts. There remains a belief by some that only boys can be Autistic, since historically that was held to be the truth. It was substantiated, amongst other things, by the larger number of boys diagnosed compared to girls. Studies vary, but according to Kanner (1943), four males will be diagnosed for every female[5]. However, based on more recent research and the growing understanding of Autism in females, it is now recognised that the 4:1 in no way reflects true gender prevalence rates, and there is a catalogue of reasons behind the gender inequalities in Autism.

Firstly, the tools created for Autism assessment were developed with boys in mind, and for establishing a diagnosis in boys. They are seeking out the male Autistic phenotype. I present a female phenotype of Autism. Generally speaking, boys are more likely to 'act out' and their behaviour flagged up early in education. Learning disability is also more statistically prevalent in Autistics, at 40% compared to the 1% in the general population[6]. Those with an additional learning disability, such as my brother, were likely to be identified sooner. Autistics who are non-verbal or have speech and language difficulties would also be identified sooner, but it should be noted that non-verbal does not automatically imply the presence of a learning disability. There are plenty of examples of highly intelligent non-verbal Autistic people. These Autistic people simply communicate through alternative media, for example writing, like the Autistic writer Naoki Higashida who authored *The Reason I Jump*[7]. One of the challenges with Autistic girls is we learn to 'socially mask' our impairments very quickly, often as infants. We recognise we are different, so we mimic to fit in. For me this started around the age of three or four. I was umbrella picking at the age of three because I hadn't yet learned to hide my Autistic traits, and when Mum was around I felt safe to be myself. Picking detritus up from the floor is one of my Autistic traits – OCD tendencies – that I hide when others are around. At the age of three, however, I was beginning to recognise a difference between me and my female peers and my inability to interact comfortably with them. At four I had started to hone my 'social masking' craft. As it turned out, this was to be both a blessing and a curse. I have survived because I learned to do it quickly, and to do it well, yet I have suffered and been missed because of this. There is also presumption that girls with Autism do not get diagnosed because we are not suffering, or we have our problems under control or managed. This is not true; our suffering is simply hidden behind a mask, the pain buried.

I believe one of the other big challenges for girls (social masking is more common amongst girls), especially girls and women who mask, is that we start to develop comorbidities (comorbid) mental health problems as a result of the façade, and once we satisfy the criteria for a mental health diagnosis, we become quickly absorbed into the mental health system and remain lost in there. Girls are very often labelled with conditions such as anxiety disorders, diagnoses like generalised anxiety disorder (GAD), PTSD and complex or C-PTSD, social anxiety, and obsessive-compulsive disorder (OCD). Lost people receive diagnoses of mood disorders like bipolar disorder and depression, and personality disorders such as emotionally unstable personality disorder, previously referred to as borderline personality disorder. I caveat that with the fact that it is, of course, possible to have these diagnoses and not be Autistic, and vice versa. Girls very often present with co-existing signs of distress in the form of eating disorders, self-harm and addiction. Based on my reading and reflections to date, I would personally go so far as to say we should consider screening every single girl, and every single boy who identifies as LGBTQIA+ (lesbian, gay, bisexual, transgender, intersexual, queer/questioning, non-binary, asexual, pansexual, and others) and has an eating disorder for Autism. The crossover here appears to be exceptionally high. But that would make sense because a common factor in those experiencing these signs of distress is low self-esteem. These people *would* have low self-esteem if they don't know *who* they are. Identification is essential given one of the most important parts of supporting someone with an eating disorder is to help them to build their self-esteem. I make no apologies for reiterating my earlier point – you cannot build self-esteem if you do not know *who* you are. Finding those with eating disorders who are autistic could become essential to their survival. It's possible healthcare could be wasting a vast amount of resource on ineffective treatment because we don't fully understand a patient's aetiology. I would advocate finding those people as part of treating their condition. If they are lost, finding them could determine the likelihood of the intervention being effective. We are currently offering interventions to people who cannot build the necessary self-esteem that will help the interventions for eating disorders (and/or addiction) to be effective. I should reiterate that it is possible to have a mental ill-health diagnosis such as an eating disorder or addiction and not be Autistic, and likewise it is possible to be Autistic and not have an eating disorder.

I believe another fundamental issue is that mental health professionals with the clinical qualification to diagnose, such as psychiatrists, are generally not taught to be Autism aware/alert, they have been taught to be mental health aware/alert, so in nearly every case they miss the fundament because they are not aware to look for it. The related gap in knowledge also means they will not likely recognise the benefits of finding it. We find what we look for, do we not? And, in my experience, and others I have witnessed, how much money or effort you throw at clinical professionals does not increase the likelihood of finding your truth. Whether you receive NHS care, or private care, professionals in neither provision seem to have been given sufficient training in Autism. There are some exceptions, but they are rarer than they are common. It is a glaring omission that is costing healthcare millions, and if changed, could *save* it millions, and more importantly, save lives! Finding your neurological truth is an intervention that has the power to improve mental health outcomes exponentially. Given the above, the 1:57 (1-2%) diagnosed Autistic[8] is likely to be an underestimate, especially in females. My anecdotal experience since diagnosis tells me this figure is likely to be significantly less than the reality. Imagine the changes in health outcomes if we were to find lost people and provide treatments appropriate to their aetiology.

A recent Channel Four TV documentary[9] about Autism

highlighted research undertaken in the last few years by Simon Baron-Cohen, British Clinical Psychologist and Professor of Developmental Psychopathy at the University of Cambridge, which included a survey of 750,000 adults across the UK. The aim of the research was to establish how autistic traits are spread out across the population and to assess theories regarding a 'lost generation' of Autistic adults. Of 750,000 people completing the survey, 87,000 met the cut-off criteria for a diagnosis of Autism (11.6%). Further still, of the 87,000 who met this, 47,000 (54%) were women. This is the generation of women now referred to as 'The Lost Girls' of which I am one, albeit I have been found. This data supports my own anecdotal experience and is in fact a little higher than my personal perception, which I felt was around 10%. My belief, in part based on my work in mental health, is that many of these people are currently lost in the mental health system, some never to be found. Because of the suffering lost women (and men) experience, sadly some of these individuals will not survive at all. And the biggest tragedy is that it would not take too much change and understanding to find them. At the time of writing, Autism is the only condition in the UK with its own legislation, the Autism Act 2009[10], and every five years or so the government brings out a new strategy, including commitments as to how it will support Autistic people. It documents financial investment, who it aims to support, and now includes children as well as adults with Autism. Local authorities and the NHS are required to consider the strategy and apply it on a local level. Each council has an Autism Lead and an Autism Partnership Board who are accountable for this. The strategy covers health, education, employment, awareness, equality, and inclusion. This is good news for people with Autism, but it is of little help to those who remain unidentified and lost. With the aforementioned challenges, it is perhaps unsurprising that when the general public talk about Autism it can often be in a misinformed way. Many will question whether they should now refer to me as 'a person with Autism' or 'a person suffering from Autism' or 'a person who has Autism'. The latter is typically used in the way we describe someone who has a mental health condition to avoid labelling them, for example, 'a person with schizophrenia' rather than 'a person who *is* schizophrenic'. We try to avoid reducing people down to a diagnosis because they have lots more facets to their identity than just being a diagnosis. But in respect of Autism, most people in the Autistic community prefer to refer to themselves as Autistic: "My name is Jane McNeice, and I am Autistic." This resembles other types of identity-first descriptors. For example, we would never say a person identifying as black and minority ethnic '*has* Asian', no they *are* Asian, or someone identifying as LGBTQIA+ '*has* gay', no they *are* gay. You *are* Autistic, not have, not suffer from, not with, but ARE. It is our identity, our difference, not something we carry around like an accessory, and not something that is bad. Some Autistic people will refer to themselves as neurodiverse or neurodivergent and refer to people without Autism or other neurodiversity as neurotypicals – NDs and NTs – or allistic, the latter referring to non-Autistic people. I will use the term neurotypical from here on in, with some reference to allistic where relevant.

Many neurotypicals misrepresent Autistic people as being high or low functioning Autistic. In fact, the Autistic community largely prefers not to use such labels, with the odd exception, which I tend to find is those who would self-identify as *high* functioning, falling into the superiority trap rather than difference. I am yet to hear an Autistic person self-identify as being a 'low functioning' Autistic. One of the reasons for this is because functioning is not static, and low functioning could suggest a lesser type of person with Autism, and that is simply not the case. No one is lesser, or even lesser or more Autistic, we are simply different Autistic people. Neurodiversity is not just about acknowledging different brain types; it is about accepting that no one brain type is superior to another. Neurodiverse language used by the public does not as yet reflect this.

The degree of challenge and level of disability someone's Autism can present is also different. High and low functioning paradigms of Autism can also infer that Autism is a single continuum, one line, and that too is not the case. There are dimensions, or facets on the Autistic Spectrum. Imagine a colour wheel and replace some of the colours with labels like 'language', 'social skills', 'perception', 'sensory', 'environmental sensitivities' and 'executive functioning'. Each of these facets could be measured on a zero to ten, zero at the centre of the wheel, ten at the perimeter, and if you were to measure each

Autistic person against each of these, you would in fact end up with a shape looking much more like a constellation of stars – a spiky profile, even – beautiful in its own unique way. This also explains why:

"If you've met one person with Autism, you've met one person with Autism."

Dr Stephen Shore (2018)[11]

We are individually different Autistic people, often incredibly so, but we share common traits that satisfy clinical criteria that define us jointly as Autistic.

I am very aware of how volatile my own functioning is. If I were to even try to measure it on a one-line continuum of zero to ten, ten being high functioning, zero being low, on a good day when I am clear and eloquent (scripting without stammering), and 'firing on all cylinders', I am a ten. I am self-aware enough to recognise myself as a ten on these days, and you'll likely hear me say things like, "Gosh! If I could just bottle that for the rest of the time!" But I cannot, because in other situations, on other days, I am a two. Put me in a social situation with strangers where I feel intimidated, or where there are dominant or prickly characters, or even when a level of spontaneity is required from me (Autistics need time to process, we struggle with spontaneity unless you are asking about our obsessions, in which case we are often encyclopaedic in our response), my functioning drops and it drops fast. I become very anxious and non-verbal, I simply observe and think, and very

Conversations

often beat myself up for not being able to communicate – or communicate effectively – like everyone else. I will then ruminate over my inept communication for a length of time afterwards. It is stored in the archive of little 't' traumas, resurfacing sometime in the future as a reminder of my ineffective social communication skills. I will feel frustrated because non-verbal does not mean having nothing to say. But the measure I am using is a neurotypical one and that is faulty for me. I use a neurotypical standard because, despite being neurodivergent, I have spent forty-five years trying so hard to pretend I am neurotypical, I have internalised measures that do not belong to me. I should in fact be measuring myself by an Autistic standard tailored just for my Autistic profile, and if I did so, I would in fact be 'normal' for me.

High and effective levels of communication are the 'gold standard' in our society, created by neurotypicals and extroverts, and revered by the same. Those standards were never built to accommodate Autistic people, or people with difference. The developed world has not been designed for us, or with us. The measures therein should not be my barometer. Yet at face value, to others, I look like I am winning at life. I am a wife, a parent, a post-graduate, a successful business owner, a writer, a marathon runner. I have a high IQ of 129 and I can hold my own in a social group (through exhaustive efforts of social masking), so to the untrained eye I look like what others might still describe as 'high functioning'. But make no mistake, I am not, and I struggle, daily. My façade and other people's failure to recognise this as such, to get behind the mask, means I have not received the support when I have so desperately needed it. Through masking and working incredibly hard to achieve what many neurotypicals will find much easier, I have engineered an illusion that has been to my long-term detriment.

Another misnomer amongst neurotypicals is, "Well, we are all on the spectrum somewhere," or, "We are all a bit autistic." If we were, then Autism would not exist as an entity, it would not need to. This again is ill-informed yet given credence by the masses. You cannot be a 'little bit' Autistic, you either are, or you are not. Being a little bit Autistic would be like saying, I am a bit bloated and a bit nauseous, so I am pregnant. You either are, or you are not, there is no 'little bit' about it. Furthermore, notions of a 'little bit', whether related to Autism, obsessive-compulsive disorder or bipolar disorder (and I have heard it said of all), take people's pain and suffering and invalidate it. They reconvene us with the majority, and the majority we are not. For me personally, there is a sense that I earned the right to satisfy something clinical, some type of difference criterion, because this crap I have experienced all my life does not appear to be happening to everyone else. For a long time, I did not recognise that. I told myself everyone's life is hard, my ship is not blacker than theirs, I must simply be doing it (life) wrong. It's my fault, and the deficit is me. Now I am not for a moment saying other human beings do not experience suffering, we all do, but I've now learned that diagnoses like Autism and the symptoms therein make life (which can already be difficult) even more difficult for those who have them, whether diagnosed or not. So 'little bit' stings, it offends, and it makes little of our pain. And put simply, the facts do not back it up.

My brain is wired differently to most people's in society, or as translated so helpfully for me by a member of an online support group, "Neurotypicals are Microsoft, you are Linux." The latter is an open-source computer operating system, which can be tailored. It is less used overall compared to Microsoft, and less understood, but not less good. So, you might be wondering, how did my brain become Autistic? How does it become Linux and not Microsoft? The Autistic brain is one that develops on a different trajectory to most. The condition is largely a genetic one (approximately 80% genetic, 20% other, depending which piece of research you explore, and it appears to be an extensively researched area), with at least one close relative also likely being Autistic, often one of the parents. Only last week did I see someone on Twitter advocating that if a child is Autistic both parents should be offered screening. My personal view is it would certainly make finding 'lost people' more likely. Hans Asperger was a strong believer that Autism was passed down. There are some environmental causes too, though my personal take on the environmental causes is that they tend to relate to factors that have an impact on foetal development. For example, pollution and chemicals that mum is exposed to entering the intrauterine environment – infectious diseases, substances used by parents, etc. So, whilst they are

THE umbrella PICKER

not genetic per se, they are biological factors in the foetal sense, rather than environmental in what I myself would think of as 'learned behaviours'. Chances are, if you have Autism in your family tree, that Autism gene, or as I like to call it, the Au-some gene, is passing down, across, and wherever it sees fit, as is the case in my own family tree.

I am sure Autism runs through the maternal lineage of my family tree, and I know this because of the way I peel vegetables! I do this differently to other people, and on several occasions other people have looked at me strangely as I do this. I peel vegetables in what I see as a logical way, but I recognise others don't share my logic. I use a knife not a vegetable peeler, I drag it towards me rather than away, taking a sizable layer from the vegetable. None of this scratching endlessly at the surface with a vegetable peeler, flicking bits of skin everywhere. Yes, I lose some produce, but I can peel vegetables much more quickly this way. I do the same with all vegetables. Mum does too. I learned it from her, and she learned it from her mum, and so on and so forth. It is a product of learned Autistic logic and our Autistic resistance to change. Vegetable peelers were invented in 1947, so my grandmother would have been well used to not having one by this date and would have been unlikely to change what she already knew worked well for her. Someone further up the tree used Autistic logic and that's how I know it goes back generations in our family. Don't they always say: to understand the present we should understand our past. I've talked to Mum about the female lineage. We've talked about the fact that Mum's

24

maternal grandmother, my great-grandmother, would not leave the home and was diagnosed agoraphobic. On reflection, my own late grandmother was very similar to me in traits – perfectionist, anxious, over-working and meticulous in so many ways. Like Mum, she also feared medical care and did not access healthcare at the earliest opportunity when she needed it, which in the end likely contributed to her young death at the age of fifty-eight. Only through analysing the past together can we now see the undiagnosed presence of autism and how it has had an impact on both our present and the past. For years I have felt a conscious, almost spiritual, responsibility to break a negative pattern within our family tree, but I was never able to identify what it was that I was to change. I now recognise it was to break the chain of undiagnosed autism in our family tree.

I had now shared with those close to me that I was Autistic. I knew who I was and so did they, but a part of me was very conscious that my wider circle still did not know, and worse still, they only knew a mask or semi-mask at best. Other family members and friends, people from my professional past and present, associates and acquaintances, those who have a window into my world via social media, they did not know. One thing I was clear about was that I am not ashamed of who I am. How could I be ashamed of what I had searched so long for? My identity. I had a compelling need to share that with others, to help them to understand me, to understand Autism, and to aid my quest for positive change so that girls and women would be found. The only way to do that was to tell the world. So, I did. I told them in writing (with a few typos and grammatical errors as I do not edit my social media posts to the extent that I will this book) because that is how I could express myself best, and this is what I wrote:

On 3rd October I'm running the 'virtual' London Marathon for the National Autistic Society and today is my 'Coming Out' day...

On 22nd June 2021 I was diagnosed Autistic after 45 years of searching for answers to unfathomable questions and being misdiagnosed for years with anxiety disorders. I AM anxious, all of the time in fact, but that's because I am Autistic not because I am mentally ill per se. Today I am owning my Autism, and the Awesome that it also provides. I don't need you to believe in the Awesome, I just need to.

To those who I could never express how I felt to or who I walked away from because of that, whose name I forgot, or who thought I was quiet or aloof, or to those I interrupted when I tried to guess when to speak in a room full of people, these are just a few of the many parts of my Autism. Please try to understand that I've been a square peg in a round hole all my life.

As a neurodiverse person in a neurotypical world,

I was discriminated against from day one because society expects everyone to be neurotypical; I am not. I mask pretty much all of the time in order to fit in, and with most people in my life, and I have various masks (... so if you're thinking, she doesn't look autistic, well yes that's because I've spent the last 45 years crafting the art – I'm a chameleon and I'm good at it, mostly). I have to work incredibly hard to do the job I do as a trainer and running my own company, but my own suffering is what drives me to help others through my work.

Today I'm removing the mask to reveal the real me, and publicly in writing, because writing is what I find easiest and where I can express myself, and because masking is totally exhausting! Sadly, masking is also a strong predictor of suicide in Autistics, it is dangerous. I personally cannot run and mask at the same time, so I am running solo on 3rd October and will do the Marathon virtually, all 26.2 miles of it!

I'm doing this for me as part of my acceptance of being Autistic, but also to raise awareness of Autism in girls and women in the hope that we stop missing girls who are autistic because they are well behaved and quiet at school and because they are high achievers or successful. They are often the latter because of the Awesome side of Autism. If you know or support girls with relentless anxiety (or depression) please stop to question whether there is more to this person than you or they yet know, or whether the professionals have failed to find the fundamental issue. I found my own answer months earlier from a social media post describing girls with Autism, I knew immediately. It wasn't a clinical professional who found the answer, it was me, though it still required a clinical professional to medically diagnose it. It should never have taken 45 difficult years.

My other hope in raising awareness is to discourage comments like 'we're all a bit autistic' or 'well, we're all on the spectrum somewhere'. Only if 99% are at zero autism and 1% full. Such statements, often well intended, take my own and other neurodiverse people's experiences and regroup us as neurotypical, which we are clinically proven (to the required level) not to be, and many of us have fought tirelessly to prove that and to find the truth to our suffering. It's like saying we're all a bit pregnant when someone is feeling nauseous and a bit bloated. Such statements invalidate 45 years of painful searching, daily anxiety, chronic IBS, and invalidate each and every time I've felt that life is not worth living. If you believe such statements as your truth keep it for you, or maybe research it and see if it is in fact true rather than something you've heard along the way. For me it does more harm than good to my experience, but

I cannot express that to you directly when you say it because of the Autism.

If you'd like to help me on 3rd October, and all the other #lostgirls of my generation, you might like to support my fundraising for the National Autistic Society, and we all thank you in advance for your generosity 🫶 #nomorelostgirls #autism
https://www.justgiving.com/fundraising/Jane-McNeice

My 'coming out' was around three weeks after diagnosis, giving me the chance to start coming to terms with it myself first. I can only liken my compelling need to 'come out' to how it must feel to share any hidden identity with the world. For example, 'coming out' as gay or bisexual. I know the level of vulnerability that it takes to turn the inside out, the personal and professional implications that must be considered, and the level of catharsis it provides. I appreciate not everyone who is diagnosed Autistic will feel a need to 'come out', or so publicly, disclosure is after all a personal choice. For me, I felt it was a means to an end, and everything I already lived by. I have always believed that to challenge stigma, whether related to mental health, neurodiversity, or any other disability, we first need to say, "This is me," and I had already been doing that for a long time, sharing with others my lived experience of anxiety disorders. But my past disclosure was now incorrect and as an Autistic person priding honesty, I needed to correct my truth in the minds of others. I personally felt it fundamental to the next step in tackling stigma and lack of understanding in Autism. I am also aware that stigma comes in different forms, it can be self-stigma, perceived stigma, and/or actual stigma. Even if you do not self-stigmatise, you might still be very aware that 'coming out' could be career damaging because other people may still stigmatise you, regardless of any self-stigma. I had to consider whether all my business clients would still feel confident in me and my company's ability to deliver our services. That was a huge risk for me and knowing that I chose to take it anyway will likely indicate to you the level of my desire to change the future, and my need to 'own' my new identity. It was a vulnerable choice, and it is not a choice I regret. I shared my 'coming out' post on my business blog, my company e-news, which goes out to my clients, Facebook, Twitter and LinkedIn. At that point, the post became my most viewed post ever on LinkedIn, though only a small number directly acknowledged it. There will be lots of reasons behind both of these facts. People love gossip! I had given them gossip. People are generally nosey. I had given them something to nose. People want to relate to their peers. I am their peer and I had given them something that would be more, or less, relatable to them. One realisation that came from the post was that others do not really know what to say. I have family members who to this point have not acknowledged my 'coming out'. I suspect that they too do not know what to say. What would have felt nice would have been something along the lines of 'I'm pleased you have found who you are, and I'm sorry you had to suffer for so long', but that would require a level of understanding of my suffering and of my past. Not everyone knows my past. I suspect many simply do not know what the condition is about, their only reference being Raymond Babbitt from *Rain Man* from the 1980s. And let's be realistic, many will simply not care two hoots about me or my suffering, they are simply not bothered and that is that. I am okay with that; I have learned over the years to be okay with that. I have learned I will never be the most important person who walks into a room, I will hide on the sidelines where no one can see me, a chameleon. I will be quiet, tucked out of the way, at the back of photographs and videos, the person hidden in plain sight, even from themselves up until now.

CHAPTER TWO

The Umbrella Picker

On 13th February 1973, my brother Robert was born to Susan and Brian at Doncaster Royal Infirmary. On Friday 14th November 1975 I followed, a girl, marking the completion of their little family.

Mum and Dad had been married on 6th November 1971 at St Jude's Church in Hexthorpe. They had been dating for approximately three years prior to their marriage, meeting at ages seventeen and eighteen respectively, young loves of their time. November 2021 will mark their fifty-year Golden Wedding anniversary, one that few marriages will ever see.

Mum was a state-enrolled nurse prior to having her children. She chose to give up her career to become a full-time mum, something in the longer term she would come to regret – the career not the mum bit (I hope!) – but she did occasionally work part-time supporting adults with special needs. She does not judge disability nor vulnerability. When Mum is around those with the greatest needs, her most beautiful gifts become apparent, just like they did in Robert. She has a big heart but battles a life without her own truth, a life marred by many kinds of loss.

Following their wedding, Mum moved in with Dad, relocating from central Doncaster with her parents to a small town nearby called Thorne. They have lived in the same property ever since. In the seventies, this would have been a significant move, particularly as neither could drive and they did not own a family vehicle. This was typical of an era when many families still relied heavily on public transport, and it cost something ridiculously little like two pence to travel on a bus!

Robert and I grew up during the eighties on a small council estate in Thorne, living in an unusual flat-roofed property, characterised by a leaky roof, which Mum struggled to cope with. There was often a bucket catching water and an emergency call out to Thorne Town Council or Doncaster Metropolitan Borough Council. Over the years, the local authority addressed the leaky roof issues, and over time many tenants exercised their 'right to buy', which has resulted in much of the small estate now being privately owned.

Our home was typical of its time; seventies maroon leather sofa and partitioning, psychedelic carpets and extraordinarily cold rooms. At a time when most homes did not yet have central heating and were still warmed by coal fires, unless you were in the sitting room where the fire had been made and well established, the house was freezing. Central heating was not installed by the authorities until after 1994 when I had left home. Private tenants had purchased their homes and installed this sooner, but Mum and Dad chose for a variety of reasons not to purchase theirs, and Mum was extremely resistant to change. She washed clothes with a twin-tub washing machine until well into the noughties; it was what she knew and what she felt safe with.

A standard winter morning during childhood included ice on the interior of the windows and waking up seeing your breath. As a child, I always slept in the foetal position and had put this down to unconscious self-preservation, but in reality it was the warmest position to be in! I no longer need to sleep in this position. Bathtubs were not plastic in the 1980s, they were heavy enamel-coated metal baths, but once the hot water heated the tub, they retained the heat so much more efficiently than the plastic baths of today. Because the house was so cold, the bath water created high volumes of steam and left the bathroom with resistant mould problems for many years.

Despite the home economics challenges, Mum always kept a home of extremely high standard. The perfect living space is such a personal and individual thing and Mum's home was perfect to her; it still is perfect to her. Mum's ideals of perfection came, and continue to come, with a rigid and structured regimen that could not be changed for anything or anyone.

From early childhood I always remember routines; Mums' not my own at this point. A typical day started with being up at the time of Mum's convenience, usually early, regardless of the day. We were always given breakfast before school and were rarely late. After my brother and I went to our separate schools, Mum would make all the beds and clean the bathroom and toilet, both of which were separate and remain so in Mum and Dad's home today. Mum would proceed to vacuum the bedrooms, landing and stairs, and then move on to her routine for downstairs. The sitting room had 'plumbed' cushions, and sofas were protected with antimacassars and melamine cups to protect the carpets from the sofa feet. Rugs had to be lifted, vacuumed under, vacuumed over, and everything in its place. The unwritten but fully acknowledged and accepted rules of the Horton home were not to sit on the sofa (sofas were for adults), not to sit on beds once they had been made, dishes not to be left in the sink, and never *ever* to touch ornaments. In addition to the morning regimen, the home was vacuumed after each meal. Net curtains and curtains were washed weekly and re-hung. Everything had a place, and we were not to touch it or move any of it. It was Mum's haven, her safe space.

As a child you learn the household status quo and whatever that happens to be is what you live by. It is the only thing you know, and you just presume other households to be the same. But I started to learn from visiting friends' houses as I got older that this was not the case, and that I was growing up in quite a unique environment with a mum who required extreme levels of order and control. Mum's regimen continues today, and she views this as 'house proud' and nothing more. Mum was comfortable when Dad, Robert and I were out of the way and giving her the space to do what she needed to. She needed alone time. Robert and I spent a lot of time out in all weathers. Interestingly, I am more than okay when out running in all weathers today. Perhaps my tolerance was developed young. The one part of Mum's obsession that I constantly challenged, however, was why I could never have friends over to play in my bedroom, in my space, and why I could not have a home birthday party with friends just like all the other children. Friends (and their parents by proxy) often asked why I was permitted to sleep over at their house, but they were never invited to sleep over at mine. Mum would never allow it, despite my attempts. Explaining this to my friends became impossible; I simply could not provide an answer, and I could not defend Mum. I had no explanation for the 'why'.

In my adult years, I came to view Mum's behaviour as an indicator of rejection and that she did not love me enough. I now know this is not true. Mum's need for order and routine means that we are not, and have not, been able to visit as regularly as the children and I would like. She is unable to cope with visits. Today I understand it differently, because today I know that this regimen is Mum meeting her very basic needs, one of her obsessions, and without it she would not and could not have survived.

Imagine Maslow's hierarchy of needs[12]. Our basic human needs are physiological needs, for example food, breathing, sleep. We then step up to safety needs, which include security, morality, health, etc. Mum's obsessions, and my own for that matter, link to these foundational steps, they form part of our very basic needs. They are an inherent part of an Autistic person's survival. Maslow's hierarchy of needs looks different when you apply it to an

Autistic person because we have basic needs not typically seen in neurotypicals, which we must prioritise to survive. Many of the evidence-based psychological models, health promotion tips and advice, life quotes, etc., have been developed by neurotypicals with neurotypicals in mind. If they were developed by Autistic people for Autistic people, they may look very different. I am now questioning everything in the psychological sciences that I previously believed to be true. A model which works for neurotypicals may be highly faulty for neurodiverse people, and some interventions often force neurodivergent people to be neurotypical – square pegs and round holes! These things need to be adapted if they are to effectively meet the needs of the neurodiverse population. With Mum it was *never* the case that I was being rejected or was not loved, it was more the case that she had to satisfy her own obsessive needs *in order* to get to the next level of loving me and my brother. I understand that now.

This is just one example of a part of my life that became detoxified on the back of my own diagnosis. The relationship between Mum and myself is already improved. What I now understand is that Mum is also autistic. It explains why she had, and still has, five vacuum cleaners, all in good working order, but all satisfying a safety and security need that she has. Mum and I have discussed the option of formal diagnosis, but her view is that there is nothing that can be done to help her now, it is too late. Mum turned seventy in September 2021; she will remain a lost girl, but no longer lost to me.

Once Mum had met her basic needs, she could be warm, loving and caring, and she was. I have fond memories of snuggling up next to her on the sofa, when permitted to gravitate from the floor, of course. And we must never bounce on the sofa, and *definitely* no sitting on the arm! "You will break the arm!" I have never yet seen a sofa with a broken arm, yet mum is not the only person I have heard say this. Maybe I have not seen it because we have *all* been told never to sit on sofa arms!

When I was with Mum, I felt safe, but I also felt scared. At the age of three, I started to have recurring nightmares of Mum and I walking down the alleyway behind the house, referred to locally as 'the snicket'. In the snicket, Mum was wearing a purple coat and a long green woollen scarf, all a bit Joker-esque. Memories of her at this time always featured the coat and the scarf, they were her signature, the scarf she always wore to cover her mouth because she was undergoing some variety of barbarous dental treatment. By the age of twenty-four, Mum had all but six teeth removed at the hands of the local dentist. This predates a time when dentists would save what they could, perhaps fortuitously in respect of future treatment on those teeth and the long-term return on investment. Mum had her gums torn and was in constant and significant pain. She was vulnerable, she communicated her fear hysterically, and it resulted in me also feeling vulnerable. In my dream, gaping holes would emerge in the snicket floor and large snakes would take her from me. I tried to save her from being pulled away, but I could not. I used to wake crying and frightened.

I now believe the recurring dream to be about insecurity and perhaps an internalisation of Mum's fear in relation to her dental treatment. I think a part of me thought she would die, and I would lose her forever.

My first detailed childhood memory was of being two years old. I now put the fact that I can remember memories from such an early age down to my Autism. Autistic people tend to have exceptional long-term memories. Prior to my diagnosis, I thought everyone could remember being the age of two, but it turns out this is not the case for most people. In the memory I was playing on a wooden climbing frame, about to go down an adjoining slide in a small church hall at the Methodist church in Thorne. I was with Mum and my older brother Robert. From the age of three onwards I have even more incredibly detailed memories, and it is from these that I start to recall secondary memories, emotional memories.

Memories comprise cognitive *and* emotional parts. Having a great long-term cognitive memory can be helpful – I can recite near four thousand words verbatim if given twenty-four hours to memorise them, as illustrated in my seen exams at university, which I will talk about later in the book – but I also have a great long-term memory for emotions, including negative feelings, and the latter can be the downside. If the memory is negative, I am quite simply re-traumatised (mostly with a little 't') by the emotional memory as well. Memories that I recall come with a flood of strong negative emotions, be that pain, anger, elation, suffering (particularly because of the impact of my undiagnosed autism), and so on. I *feel* the memory, as well as recall the memory cognitively, and I feel it as if it's re-happening, and on a physical level. It is fair to say that neurotypicals will experience this too, but what I am trying to convey is the amplified level at which Autistics experience this, and the higher likelihood that it will be negative rather than positive. But just like neurotypicals, I also have positive memories, songs, holidays and the positive feelings that go with those. A song memory can trigger me into what feels like euphoria, an unnatural high of feelings.

A lot of my memories from the age of three take me back to being at Green Top nursery school in Thorne, so called because of its green roof tiles – no need for over-complicating things! I think someone once told me it was to camouflage the building during the war. How true that is I do not know. I remember the smell of the malted milk biscuits we were given, and the smell of hops from the old Darley's Brewery in Thorne. I remember outdoor playtime, often playing on a trike of some kind and often playing alone. In the nursery indoor play area, there was a dressing up box, and Mum had kindly donated her wedding dress for the little girls to play dress up. I'm pretty sure there would have been boys who would have liked to dress up in it too, boys who were learning to mask *their* truth, and those who were as yet, gender blind. I recall watching from the quiet corner, seeing the little girls putting on the dress and thinking '*but I* want to wear it, the dress belonged to *my* mum', but I did not assert that or try to get involved. I was too frightened and timid. Instead, I sat picking up books and looking through the pages. Books and words were already starting to reveal themselves as something that would comfort and save me. I simply did not know how to socially engage. I would reciprocate if others engaged with me, but I was extremely quiet and reserved, holding back otherwise (just like I do today). Today the vibe I give off could be seen as aloof. I have known that for a long time. I am also aware that others sometimes view me as 'stuck-up', believing I look down on them – they are so wrong, how could I? I am always clean, well presented, well dressed, full make-up, and bejewelled. People make judgements all the time, and my appearance, like any, is open to this. If, by chance, we eventually engage, or even become friends, people often reveal that when we first met, they thought I was 'stuck up'. They affirm a perception I notice at the time. It often comes out by way of a retrospective apology; they were wrong for thinking it because they now know I am not. Autistic people are far less likely to judge than neurotypicals, maybe because we always recognise ourselves as being 'outsiders' or the 'odd one out'. When you are an observer of the world rather than a participant, you feel in no place to judge. Autistics are so often acutely aware of others' judgement of them, so why would we ever want to do that to someone else?! Hey, I am no angel, I *have* formed judgements, but I am aware of it, and I chastise and challenge myself when it happens. Being Autistic does not give you a clean slate and render you judgement free, but it does make you more aware of the unnecessary suffering caused by judgement. You constantly challenge yourself to be a better person.

I recall the little 't' trauma of Mum removing my dummy and burning it one night (the harsh extraction method!) and the transition from Green Top Nursery to Fieldside First School, my new primary school. I recall seeking lots of reassurance from Mum: "Who will be in my class? What if they are not? Will it be easy? What if I don't like it?" Mum always reassured, though I sensed she was frightened both *for* me, and *with* me. I started primary school in 1979, and hated it from there on in, or at least the people part – mostly the discomfort of being with other children – but I loved the learning, and I was good at it. Since I feared other children, I gravitated towards the adults – dinner ladies with whom I sought comfort and conversation, and teachers, though I was exceptionally frightened of authority and communicated through whispering and disproportionate levels of subservience. Autistic girls often learn to believe that if they are incredibly good, people will like them, and all will be well. This being 'incredibly good' was not mirrored at home. Mum would often say, "She is a little bugger at home," which I now understand as the so called 'four 'o clock explosion'[13] often witnessed in Autistic children who mask at school and drop the façade when they come out, being themselves and letting out all that has been hidden and suppressed during the day! If an Autistic child is down-masking with you, there is good reason to believe they feel safe with you. Autistic meltdowns, challenging as they are,

are a sign that the Autistic person feels they can, or they simply cannot hold it anymore, no matter what or who you are. They have reached melting point.

From the age of three, I could tie shoelaces. The middle-aged dinner ladies found it invaluable that I could save their backs and tie the children's shoelaces on command, and I loved it because I knew it made them happy. What I did not recognise was that this was one small part of the bedrock that would become me being a people-pleaser. I was already aware that I did not fit in, especially amongst my peers. Some of the girls were bossy and pushed me about, shoving me out of queues to push in front. I did not know what to say or do, so I just moved to the back or let them go first. I was quite literally a pushover and was already showing signs that I was socially unable to defend myself. I would sit in classrooms having forgotten to take off my coat, like Fieldside First School's answer to *Coronation Street*'s Roy Cropper, always feeling cold and always feeling scared. A combination of anxiety and autistic executive functioning issues caused me short-term memory problems, and they still do. I would sit frozen, frightened to the point of panic, unable to breathe, thinking *I need to take my coat off but I daren't. If my teacher sees me with my coat on, I am going to get into trouble, and if she sees me leave the room, I am going to get into trouble.* Damned if I do, damned if I don't. Eventually, I would move beyond frozen and immobility, walk to the cloakroom, take off and hang up my coat. I would then make my stealth-like return to the classroom. This fear of getting into trouble, over-subservience and inability to express my needs to grown-ups found me having to wear other people's donations on several occasions – usually trousers since the pretty dresses did not fit my tall frame as I was bigger than all my peers – because I had literally stood and urinated rather than saying to a grown up that I needed the toilet. One dinner lady had said, "Just wait there while I go to the loo," so I did, but I needed it too. Too late! Mum knew the moment I came out of class in red 1970's flares that another 'accident' had happened.

At the age of six, I was asked by my teacher to go and collect some fresh chalk from a class across the hall. I needed to go to the toilet. I did not dare ask to go to the toilet at the same time, as I had been given specific instructions – rules! I took them literally and did not deviate, but I still needed the toilet. I would have become the type of young apprentice who accepted, without question, the unkind initiation of being sent to ask for a left-handed sweeping brush or screwdriver! The chalk I collected had a factory coating on it that meant that it did not write, so I was sent back to the other classroom for an alternative, *still* needing the toilet. I'd held my bladder for one round, but there was no way it could withstand two! I stood for the second time in front of a class of children while the teacher fished around in her chalk box, and I urinated. That teacher would have walked back to a puddle right in the centre of her classroom floor at the front of her class. No one ever discussed it with me. To have understood that occurrence, and others, could have been enough to find me at the age of six. My teacher got her chalk.

The following year, I was placed under the tuition of the 'chalk-gate' teacher. I was now thoroughly petrified of her, and yet she had done nothing wrong. I cried every day from September through to Easter. I remember a girl called Heather Perfect mothering me, often the case with Autistic girls. We are often mothered in infant school, bullied in high school. Heather helped me with learning how to tell the time. We had been issued little orange stencil clocks to draw into our textbooks. All the blue lines of my textbook where wobbly from dripped tears. Heather doesn't know this, but I owe her a debt of gratitude for that year; she reduced my emotional pain tenfold. To this very day, in September every year, I still feel the onset of autumn through the same emotional memories I had of that school year, me sitting in assembly and feeling so incredibly sad and depressed. The emotional memory is imprinted. I was seven years old, and I was depressed. Ideas that children so young cannot be depressed are misunderstood – I was most certainly depressed. I just wanted my mum to hold me and keep me safe from people. At this point, she was a dinner lady in the school I attended, so at lunchtime I clung to her and did not want to go back into class. I was experiencing separation anxiety on a daily basis. I eventually had to prise myself away from her. The daily crying resulted in me eventually being summoned to the headteacher's office, who sat me on his knee (that would never happen today!) and asked what was wrong. Did I not like my teacher? I thought I was in trouble, so I told him I was fine, and that I did like her. Neither were true. I never cried again.

In hindsight that teacher was most likely *not* scary, bad, or otherwise, maybe strict and shouted a little, but for me that was enough. I cannot cope with that. I fear getting into trouble and it is common in Autistic people. I had also likely anchored the trauma of my 'accident' in this classroom the previous year with the same teacher. She did, however, kick-start my love of reading and stories. Last thing every day she read to us all, and she loved Roald Dahl. She read every single Roald Dahl book to us over the course of a year; she did the voices, the mimicry, and she took me away from the classroom to a place where I was no longer frightened and where I could be totally comfortable. *Fantastic Mr Fox* was my favourite, and I went on to read this book well over one hundred times during my childhood.

In times of panic, such as those highlighted, I have what I can only describe as an out of body experience. I also have what I call my existential emotion, a wave of feeling that comes over me where I near completely detach from myself and ask, "How am I me? How did I get to be me? What if I were to become someone else for a moment? How would I live their life? What would I need to remember? Will I know where I live? Where are my keys?" It is sometimes a feeling that I do not fit into the family I am living in. I have experienced this since childhood, but it still happens today. "Why did God make me ME? How did I carry my babies in my tummy, conjoined by a cord, yet I could not read their mind when, at the time, we were one?" Yes, I too recognise these thoughts as being just as strange as they sound, and I now put them down to my overthinking brain and a diffuse sense of self, as much as any existential questioning. I have since learned this diffuse sense of self is common in Autistic people, one of the very reasons undiagnosed autism can so easily become misdiagnosed with mental health problems comprising similar symptoms. Such thoughts shared with the wrong psychiatrist at the wrong time could easily move you towards a misdiagnosis of a serious mental health condition. As could the fact that throughout my life I've had occasions when I've felt a euphoric even spiritual sense of elation, and then times when my mood is in the gutter. That information in the wrong hands could look like bipolar disorder, another common misdiagnosis placed on undiagnosed autistic people. Yet they are all features of my Autism, and nothing else.

Like all children, I loved toys – in equal measure to books. I had collections! These included Sindy dolls, Barbies, erasers, stationery, and other paraphernalia that took my interest. I had an ample collection of teddies, which I took turns sleeping with each night well into my teens. No teddy would ever feel left out and alone on my watch. We had a teddy rota, oh yes we did! Mum always took me shopping with her on a Saturday afternoon, and I was confident I could manipulate her into purchasing some toy I had got my eye on. I was very suggestive, a marketer's dream, and of course there were enough TV ads in the eighties to hook me in. I think Mum also knew she would get some peace and quiet if I was occupied with a new toy. I had lots of dolls, and lots of accessories, cars, caravans and suchlike to go with them. However, one thing

I could never understand was once I had so perfectly set up their living environment and put the right clothes on the dolls, I lost interest, I did not play further. I was a 'setter upper' but not a player. I now know this relates to my lack of social imagination; I did not know *how* to socially play the characters because I lacked the social skills required to do it. An Autism aware observer would have likely made the connection between my play and my being Autistic. I was happiest in our home garden, playing on our swing, with a jumper on my head pretending I had the long hair I so desperately wanted. At those times I was a princess in her castle, waiting for her prince, waiting to be rescued. I now know it was never a prince I was waiting for, it was myself.

Summer evenings I would play 'spinning tops' or 'dizzy dollies' on the crescent green where we lived, spinning round and round. This made me feel most alive in the warm evening sunshine. As an adult this became spinning office chairs and something I've never really grown out of, or at least not until my migraine years, which started in 2007. My first bad migraine was on holiday in Bulgaria – the initiator, the one which set the trend, when little men climbed inside my head and beat my brain with hammers for three days solid and all I could do was close my eyes and try not to vomit. Later came the flashing light migraines, the auras. Today they typically present as what my mother-in-law calls 'silent migraines' – sneaky migraines with all the usual symptoms except pain. They occur when I am feeling stressed and are often triggered by physical stressors such as too much noise, cold, snow or sunlight, or things that make me feel dizzy, so no more spinning, or Waltzers at the fairground, something I loved as a teenager.

It was apparent by this time that I was different, and to the trained eye that I was struggling in a way that was different to my peers. Social interaction was my biggest challenge and I had but a small group of friends, often most comfortable one-to-one than in groups. Three was always a crowd, and three was when the bullying and ill treatment started. I generally find that even nice human beings can sometimes become unpleasant when in groups. They lose the inhibitions that are present when they are solo, a bit like the confident antelope safe amongst a thousand other antelopes. In groups I would be weeded out, subtly, but weeded out nevertheless. All the same I had found something that would set me apart, I was an academic, and I was good at it. If all else failed, I could be intelligent. I could please my teachers, my parents, and others through a high standard of schoolwork. That and my lack of good looks would later earn me the nickname 'Plain Jane Super Brain' like Jane Mangle on the popular Australian soap *Neighbours*. I was a high achiever, and I was an incredibly determined one at that. If A was the top, I wanted an A+. If 100% was the top, I wanted 101%. It is like I took the best of neurotypical standards and told myself to go one above in order to hide in plain sight. This manifestation is perfectionism. I have been doing it ever since, and I spend a lot of time trying to internalise healthier counterbalanced ideas of 'good enough'. In school, this standard of high performance secured me a place in set one in all subjects, though I started to collapse in maths at the age of ten.

At the age of ten, the maths stepped up a notch and my maths brain could not resolve the puzzles put to me. Evidence of my inability with numbers was in fact seen with the clocks at age seven. It took me a long time to learn to tell the time. I dropped from set one to set three over the course of the next five years. I left school with a GCSE grade E in mathematics. I was never assessed for the condition dyscalculia – a learning disability that affects a person's ability to comprehend numbers and simple number-based operations – but my personal view is I may have this condition as well as Autism. It is common to have more than one co-existing neurodivergence. I have no desire to go down the route of formal assessment for dyscalculia because I see no benefit. I get by. I manage money, business cashflow and budgets, and I can work out percentages and produce basic evaluations of my work. I fall in research when we get into things like standard deviation. Beyond this, I need help, but otherwise no amount of study or diagnosis is going to change the fact that my brain struggles with numbers. I undertook a foundation mathematics course in 2012 believing that it would help, but it did not really improve things. Despite me being poor with numbers, I do not struggle with the theories that sit behind them, or patterns, which oddly I still regard as maths based. My Autistic superpower is in fact pattern-seeking and, when I tested my IQ as part of my personal research for this book, the report revealed superior pattern spotting, faster than 87% of the other test respondents. I think and theorise in patterns and pictures, often like the fractals of a snowflake. There are many patterns in nature and even more in human behaviour, I find. This, I believe, compensates for my lack of Theory of Mind, which I will come on to shortly.

In the past, my pattern spotting has felt like fortune-telling, and making the case for this is challenging to say the least. I then adapted my thinking a couple of years ago to believing it was simply a high level of intuition, but today I now know it as Autistic pattern-seeking. I can predict human behaviour, and my specialist subject is foreseeing conflict, honed I am sure on the back of this being my greatest fear. It is a coping mechanism for me. I can sniff out potential for conflict like a narcotics hound, way before my peers see it coming. This allows me to circumvent conflict on many levels and on many an occasion. Hey, if all else fails, I could maybe apply for a job working at GCHQ, who I have read seek out my brain type!

To give you an idea of what conflict does to me… it makes me feel suicidal, I simply cannot cope. I understand the theoretical benefits of conflict resolution skills, and the case for assertiveness, but I cannot deliver. So, effectively, I have developed a survival strategy to spot potential conflict at the earliest opportunity, which allows me to intervene and to circumvent it, and on most occasions I can, a bit like the Kofi Annan of my own little world. The times I am not able to, I become vulnerable. I then become depressed and I need to sleep. You will regularly see my own conflict prevention behaviour at play: I am amenable, agreeable, I apologise and appease. I am diplomatic and very considered in my choice of words (this book will hopefully prove testimony to that, but I already fear that it won't). I am non-antagonistic, a people pleaser, and use the charm offensive with those who are prickly. I can generally spot prickly people quickly and give them a very wide berth, but in the workplace, for example, you cannot always do this, which I guess is why I have now engineered myself a work situation where I am only exposed to prickly folk in short one-off bursts. That said, in the last seven years, my work has taught me some beautiful lessons – that *most* people are decent and kind and dealing with their own struggles, especially the prickly ones! I also find that, in nearly all cases, the people who attend our courses are society's helpers, the good sorts. The difficulty with constant adjustment is you cannot live a life of congruence; you cannot be yourself. We all need to be true to ourselves and be able to say, "I don't agree," or, "You are making me sad," or, "It really hurts me when you do that." But I cannot. I am not able to express how I feel verbally. I have been many people's punchbag, and simply internalised my truth and the guilt of not defending myself; I've buried my feelings. I have also internalised the guilt of not being able to defend my children when they have needed it. That is the hardest part. I fail to protect my babies, and two of my three children have needed it the most. I am the human doormat, but I simply do not know how to change that. Yes, Cognitive Behavioural Therapy, Dialectical Behaviour

Therapy, Interpersonal Therapy, Schema Therapy, these are all therapies that have potential to change these types of behaviour, and I have undergone some of these treatments, but they are not shown to be highly effective for Autistic people. They need to be adapted for Autistic people, and in most cases have not been. They were designed by neurotypicals for neurotypicals. I did not even know I was Autistic when I was receiving some of these interventions, and none of the therapists had been taught to be Autism aware or to understand Autism, so what chance was there of a practitioner ever saying, "Have you explored the possibility that you might be Autistic?" Or, "We may need to tailor this therapy to meet your Autistic needs."

At this point in my life I am hoping that I now have a chance at building the necessary self-esteem and self-worth to be more assertive, to protect myself from poor mental health, and to defend my children when they need it. The wonderful thing is three months post diagnosis I can already see glimmers of improved self-esteem and confidence. For the first time in my life, I believe I can, and I will. I am looking forward to the future…

As a child I was a girly girl, I still am, very much the *pinkest* of pinks. I love feathers and sparkles, make-up and flowers, and my visual brain is drawn to *anything* aesthetic and colourful! But you would not have known that to look at me as a child. Mum had cropped my shoulder-length hair at the age of three, and it was now a short boyish haircut that I hated with a passion. I was a girl, and thought 'normal' girls have long hair, so I wanted long hair. Short hair was just another identification adding to my not fitting in. This was made worse by the fact that I wore tracksuits out to play, and grown-up strangers often referred to me as a boy; "Let this little boy go first." I am a blooming girl! I, of course, did not say that as I was too frightened and too polite, so I just internalised it as another example of 'not fitting in' to *any* group, not even my gender for goodness' sake. I rarely shared with Mum what had happened with other grown-ups and how I felt, but instead constantly asked permission to grow my hair. At the age of ten, I was finally permitted to do so. I started growing the back, which morphed into a mullet – I'm chuckling as I write that – and at the age of eleven had it neatly bobbed to the same length all round, then grew it long from there. I have never gone shorter than an inverted bob ever since. I never will. I will be the grey-haired old lady with a bun, not the short shampoo and set variety.

So, as you can see, my childhood centred around not fitting in, combined with a tremendous need to belong. This was illustrated ever more in the summer of 1982.

TRIGGER WARNING: The next three paragraphs discuss sexual assault. If this is triggering, please bypass these

It was the summer of 1982. My need to fit in was extreme. I just wanted to be like all the other girls, and by now I had an awareness that I was *not* like them. I wanted long hair, patent shoes, anything pretty, and I remain similarly girly today. I no longer want bows on my shoes, but I'm partial to a diamante or two. I am mesmerised by colour, sparkle and pretty. My favourite household chore is cleaning my crystal light fittings because they incorporate all three; it is my mindfulness chore. My need to fit in was ever more emphasised by what happened to me at the age of seven.

Whilst playing one-to-one with a local boy of a similar age, he asked if he could do 'things' to me; sexual things. I said no but he continued to persuade, manipulate and cajole over a matter of weeks by saying, "If you do, I will be your boyfriend." He knew exactly the buttons to press. He could see my greatest desire.

As a child, I was not pretty. If the children at school were playing kiss-cats, the boys would say to me, "It's okay, you don't need to run, I'll never kiss you anyway, you are ugly." I was the ugly child, and I knew it. So, this boy was offering me a way to be like the other girls, to fit in, to feel liked, but he was never going to be my boyfriend, even though his persuasion eventually succeeded. It happened, I was complicit, and that made me even more vulnerable; it resulted in the same happening several times more over the course of that summer. For a lifetime, I have felt bad, wrong, dirty, guilty and ashamed of what happened that summer. The boy concerned discussed it with me a few years later, and I simply said, "It was wrong, it should not have happened." I did not want to talk about it because I had started to convince myself it had never happened; his reopening the discussion reminded me that it did. It is something that over the years I have put to the very recesses of my mind, and it was a secret I planned to take to my grave. It is no longer going to my grave because, on the back of my diagnosis, it is yet another event that has been cleansed and detoxified, and as a result I am now able to share. The first person who I needed to tell was my husband, who just like in my previous announcement, remained calm and unphased – I needed that – it was more about my need to purge than any need for a response. Disclosure took further energy out of it, like a fire fizzling out because its fuel was gone; it had lost its toxicity.

I now understand this situation within the context of my undiagnosed autism. It happened to me because I felt I did not fit in and because I so desperately wanted to. It happened to me because I was doubly vulnerable – vulnerable by way of being a child, and vulnerable as an undiagnosed autistic. That boy offered me a way in, a way to be like all the other girls, and I took it even though I knew it was wrong. As an autistic child, I took things literally and over-trusted; I believed the boy when he said he would be my boyfriend. In sharing this I am vulnerable, this is full exposure, but I do so because it illustrates some of the risks that are present for autistic children, and the lengths an autistic child may be willing to go to in order to fit in. It illustrates why we need to find autistic children, and more importantly, why we need to protect them! They are more vulnerable to abuse because they often connect better with people of a different age; for example, adults who may not have good intentions,

intentions that they will not see due to their lack of Theory of Mind, which I will come to explain further. They over-trust, they take what is said literally, and they want to please. Imagine instead that at the age of seven I had been cajoled into getting into a stranger's vehicle, someone had some puppies they'd like me to see. The child-on-child sexual abuse that happened to me was not good, but it could have been a million times worse. As I write now, I wonder about the rates of undiagnosed autism in abducted children later found killed. If we can find these children, we can better protect them; diagnosis is vital.

Everything I've read so far tells me that autistic children are at a much greater risk of exploitation of any kind, including the aforementioned factors that autistic children connect more effectively with adults than their peers and autistic children can be seen as 'easy prey'[14]. Think gang culture, think child sexual exploitation, think about the benefits of making police officers and social services more Autism aware. Just how many of the children and young people coming into their contact are undiagnosed autistics that need to be found? Finding their truth could save them from being both victims *and* perpetrators of crime.

The boy, the protagonist, was not bad; he too had been exposed to something outside of what a child of his age should have been exposed to, otherwise he wouldn't have known about sexual activity. He was not deliberately trying to hurt me. I forgive him, and I forgive me. Since diagnosis,

THE *umbrella* PICKER

Jane McNeice, age 7

one thing I have learned is that Autistic women in particular share one common experience: they have often (but not always) been abused, sexually or emotionally, and, sadly for some, both.

I rarely return to Thorne these days, in part because of that summer, but mostly because of the negative emotions attached to a number of autobiographical memories in which I felt anxious as a child. The triggers are everywhere in Thorne, and they are inextricably linked to anxiety. Those memories sit alongside the nostalgia, the nicer moments that also exist, the pleasant, safe memories that make me want to return. But the negative ones overshadow them, so my visits are rare. These triggered memories and anxious feelings remain with me for days afterwards. Trauma for

Autistic people is not 'one-off', it is daily and never-ending. Mum and Dad still live in Thorne, and are of course very important reasons I want to visit, but Mum's own autistic challenges are also reasons it can be difficult. Mum needs her space, and her routines, and our visits upset this. I understand that now, and I too find unplanned visits to my home uncomfortable. Even planned ones sometimes. If I feel I have to socially mask in my own home, my safe space, I get more anxious and begin tidying and cleaning to cope. I feel suffocated. Home is my haven, one of the few places I can totally down-mask, but not when others invade that space. I struggle with social gatherings in my home. It makes my home sound so unwelcoming, but I try equally hard for it not to be.

Knowing I did not fit in gave me the determination to do everything within my power *to* fit in. As mentioned previously, one tool to that armour was 'social masking' and I had already started to hone my craft from an early age. I am an observer, and this is beyond 'people watching', a guilty pleasure of many. This is observing at a detailed level, it is once again amplified. I am watching your eyes, facial expression, your mannerisms, the way you walk, how you respond to other people, how you carry yourself, what you measure yourself against in life, what you say and the words you choose, what you do not say, how you sing and how you dance. I will immediately assess my ability to mimic a quirky facial expression, interesting eyebrow raise, or a wink. I am even watching your handwriting! I have been known to, and will, mimic all, because watching you and being you allows me to understand, navigate, and be accepted as neurotypical by neurotypical society. I have reached a level of masking where, at times, I have even fooled *myself* that I am neurotypical. I have internalised neurotypical ideals to such an extent they feel like my own, but they are not. This trickery comes at a grave cost. It helps you to survive, but also increases your likelihood of suffering and dying. I know that may sound shocking, but I'll explain more why this is a significant risk later.

At nine years old, I moved up to Northfield Middle School, then at age thirteen to Thorne Grammar School, from a bottle-green uniform to a navy one, neither one more attractive than the other. My primary and middle schools have since been demolished due to them being dilapidated Victorian buildings with the increasing maintenance and safety costs you might expect with buildings of that era. With each transition, a greater number of feeder schools were brought together. Two primary schools merged at middle school, and three middle schools and their feeders at grammar. With each merger and transition came an increase in people, and with each increase in people, an increase in social anxiety, and the corresponding reduction in my mood. It took me at least a year on both occasions to reach acceptance of the school transition. Until then, it was incredibly difficult, and not supported in the way that we try to support transition in today's world.

I often felt very lonely and very lost. I was a depressed teenager, who socially masked and internalised her emotions. No one knew this, although I do recall one observant friend, Maria Banner, who when I was ten said, "Jane, you don't smile any more." She could see the loss of humour and the signs of depression brought about by my inability to cope with social demands and the shift from primary to middle school. She was ten years old and more mental health aware than the grown-ups of the time; she just didn't have the word for depression.

In my work today, I am constantly in awe of the knowledge and understanding young people have when it comes to mental health, which is often superior to that of some of the adults I deliver mental health training to. My teenage depression was deep, it existed from the age of ten and continued its ebb and flow throughout my teens. December 1984 was also the year I experienced my first bereavement-related loss, my late grandmother, to whom my brother and I were close and who was quickly consumed by throat cancer at the tender age of fifty-eight. Mum was devastated and would be challenged daily by the loss for years to come. Losing her mum was incredibly difficult, but losing her son three decades later, unthinkable.

CHAPTER THREE

Adolescence Can Stay Lost!

The number of times I hear people dreamily say, "If I could just go back to my teenage years..." and I think, *Oh my God no!* I cringe. Because straight away I am launched back to images of severe acne, depression, low self-esteem, emerging gastric problems, and a million other negative memories, all accompanied by those difficult emotional scars, with a few shiny positives in between.

Teenage years can be challenging for many young people, so I know I am not alone, but once again the struggles for an Autistic teenager are often amplified. We lack social instinct, and you need it to survive in the quagmire that is teenage life, especially when you grow up in a small insular town like Thorne.

Thorne is a small historical market town with a scenic canal and some picturesque walking areas, but nevertheless, it is also a socio-economically deprived area of Doncaster. It is an area of multiple deprivation and with deprivation comes social ills. South Yorkshire is not the most affluent county of the UK, but it is my home, and make no mistake, I am a proud Yorkshire girl! I am up there in liking to believe it is God's own county, and if you were to chop me in half it would probably say 'Yorkshire born and bred' through my core, just like a stick of Yorkshire rock! I am yet to find a Yorkshire person who is not proud of their home county. We are a friendly bunch – notwithstanding my own aloof presentation – loyal and protective. Sadly, some people take such things and tarnish them with hatred and prejudice. I am talking about pride, not prejudice. But it was apparent during my teenage years that there was mental ill health around me, other young people and adults, maladaptive coping behaviours such as drink, drugs, self-harm, shoplifting and sex – all coping behaviours. These people, just like me, were trying to survive.

At the age of ten, I would go to The Moorends Welfare Club on a Monday night, otherwise known as the 'Weli'. Monday night was the youth night. I went with my best friend, her sister, and her sister's older girlfriends. I remember female staff talking about inappropriate things to the older girls – French knickers being described as 'easy feelers'! I felt out of place. Where were the *real* grown-ups, the ones who made me feel safe? I felt uncomfortable by the talk and out of my depth at the age of ten. I have never been one for any female trash talk, I cannot do it. You will never hear me describe my girlfriends as bitches or dickheads. I would choke first. Attending the Weli on a Monday night was the most anxious feeling in the world, I hated it, but I did it because I was expected to, it was neurotypical. I still associate Queen's 'It's a Kind of Magic' with the emotional anxious memory of Monday nights there. Anxiety is one of the biggest challenges for many Autistic people, and I was no different. My anxiety will always be the monster which resides.

As an adolescent, I was always a big spender, I never saved a single penny. I always had a plan for how to spend money, and the plan existed before I had earned or received it. Pocket money, babysitting money – shopping made me happy, I loved the dopamine hit. I would spend right down to the last penny, then scrounge from Mum all week for snacks and other consumables. I had a taste for quality and high-end goods, a taste I still have today. Nowadays I am conscious of my propensity to spend, and I am extra careful because of it. My husband does not think I am careful enough, and fortunately does not know how many handbags and shoes 'accidents' I have had in recent years! But today I save, and I am much more careful with money. I manage my risk. One way I do this is by simply hiding money from myself with various accounts. I hoard it and have a strict budget spreadsheet for what is left.

I take a lot of solace from music, but as a teenager my music taste, just like my dress sense, was dated. This is a common theme for girls with Autism – we cannot predict current and future trends, so we look to the past for a level of predictability. I recall a friend once saying, "The lads say you dress like their mum!" Again, I was being reminded, by a friend, that I did not fit the norm. I knew they were right, but I did not know how to change it, and I considered my style classy, and what's more I liked it. As for my music taste, to this day it is eclectic, and much of it does not sit with what is regarded as 'popular'. As a teenager, 'popular music' is the gold standard of neurotypical, so when I had been into Doncaster town centre and purchased Baker Street by Gerry Rafferty at the age of fourteen, I had to hide it when my peers jumped on the bus next to me and shared the ride home. If my self-esteem had been higher, I could have ridden my music and the journey out, but as highlighted, you cannot build self-esteem if you do not know *who* you are.

Being a teenager who was, unbeknown at the time, searching, I searched in the darker side of music for my reflection, seeking affinity with The Smiths and everything Steven Morrisey, including tracks such as 'November Spawned a Monster' (I am a Scorpio by the way, so I took this as affirmation), and The Smiths' hit single 'Ask', which asserted that shyness is good, but holds us back, and we just need to ask for help. I was what others would most definitely describe as shy, but really, I was not shy, I was Autistic.

I am not averse to listening to other dark musicians from time to time, such as Nick Cave and the Bad Seeds and their album 'Murder Ballads'. Enough said. Hey, even Kylie Minogue fraternised with a little Nick Cave in their production of 'Where the Wild Roses Grow' and Kylie's own depiction of the tragic Eliza Day. In recent years, I have learned that I am more suited to 'feel good' media. I do not watch the news, I watch very little TV, only the odd bit that will make me laugh aloud on a Friday night, *Gogglebox* in the main, which also helps me to keep in touch with what's been happening in TV media over the week. My social media usage is less of the random cyber loafing of yesteryear and more purposeful nowadays, often related to my purpose.

There are just three times in any twenty-four-hour period that I will experience cessation to my anxiety and overthinking mind. One is when I am unconscious, as in sleeping, and the other two are when I read, or when I write. I am simply unable to be anxious when I read or write. So, it may come as no surprise that I am a voracious reader. I mostly read fiction, which is less common among Autistics as we often prefer factual literature, but I love the escapism that fiction provides, and I suppose the benefit that I can learn how to socialise or hone my social masking skills through fictional characters. I do not read sci-fi or fantasy, however, I simply do not connect with this genre. As a teen I had not yet recognised that reading and writing was my lifeline, but in hindsight there were signs of connection at various intervals. In recent years, my reading genre has changed. During my teenage years and the noughties, I read (a lot) of factual and fictional crime literature. I also watched a lot of TV horror. Images from both have given me intrusive thoughts that stay with me even today. It took me longer than it ought to have to recognise that this genre was not helpful for my anxiety. I no longer torture myself with either of these. Lesson learned, slowly!

Though I did not recognise it at the time, I was happiest when alone, but conditioned by the neurotypical world I was living in (but not fitting in), I forced myself to do and be neurotypical, which included socialising. I would attend the local 'Youthy', a youth club in Thorne run by middle-aged women, occasionally frequented by gym goers (there was an adjoining gym), and everyone who was cool, hip and happening. As a teen, I typically got on with both the 'in' and the 'out' crowd, and anyone in between. Of course I did, I just observed and switched the mask. But I knew without any doubt that I did not belong with either. For starters, I could not dance, and to this day cannot dance (or sing) comfortably in front of others, yet I love both. I can dance in my kitchen when my favourite tune comes on, though my kids call it my 'chicken dance', so I will let you be the judge of my prowess. I feel incredibly self-conscious when I sing or dance. Both are part of the neurotypical teenage (and adult) 'gold standard'. I never really understood the rules of the Youthy, so I stood about and talked with friends, and usually found myself buying and eating too many sugary foods from the tuck shop. Unlike school, where I knew my place and purpose for being there, navigating the Youthy was not easy. Other girls thought it cool to down straight bottles of vodka, so I thought I should do that too – oh my God, turps in a bottle! I do not touch the stuff to this day. In fact, I rarely drink at all, which I have now learned is one of my Autistic traits. I have a strong need to be in control and to socially mask. It is hard to do either when under the influence of alcohol because both need effort and effective cognition, not a brain flooded with dopamine! I have a cocktail or two when I do not have my vehicle or children with me, so essentially when I am having a weekend away with a friend via alternative transport, or when I am away with my husband without my car or other responsibilities. I have to know that the person with me can take care of me if I drop my control. I probably have less than half a dozen drinks a year. They are usually sweet and pop-like, though may contain a lot of alcohol, cocktails in the main. I am much more of a brew girl; a nice cup of decent quality tea and a book is when I am at my most content and myself. And it does not have to be Yorkshire tea! If I whisper that no one will hear it, will they?

Likewise, some of my girlfriends thought it cool to smoke, so social smoking became part of my social masking repertoire. Just one or two when out with friends who also smoked. I had no more than about twenty a year, and to the dismay of friends over the years, never purchased my own. To purchase my own would have been to cross a line that said I was 'a smoker'. I *did not* want 'smoker' as part of my identity because it wasn't the real me. I was just trying to fit in. I never smoked another cigarette following the death of my brother in 2014 of terminal bowel cancer. He was forty-one. Some people reading this will be surprised to read that I ever smoked at all, but that mask was only needed in certain social groups, and in fact would have been absolutely scorned upon in others, so you may not have seen it if you scorn smoking. It would have isolated me further in some groups, so I would simply not have done it. The unmasked me despises smoking, that is my true self. That will surprise some people too.

One of the most significant challenges during adolescence was the emergence of teenage acne from around the age of twelve. It was red, sore and explosive, and yet another reason for boys to remind me how ugly I was. I felt it, they affirmed it. I was called 'Pizza Face' and 'Spotty Muldoon'. People made jokes like, "Hey Spotty, where's Super Ted?" During adolescence I had tried every spot remedy available to my teenage budget, which consisted of babysitting money, £5 per week pocket money, and a few quid I had taken from my brother's money box and 'fessed up to years later. Fortunately, my brother took it in good humour; it was another cleansing moment for me, pardon the pun! I had tried all the 'oxy' range, which stripped my sore skin bare. I tried lotions and potions – stuff to put on me, and stuff to put in me – vitamins and detoxifiers. I drank water like a fish, in a desperate attempt to filter and flush the badness away. Nothing worked, only age in the end.

Because of the acne and social anxiety, I found any attention on me extremely uncomfortable. My eye contact was extremely poor, and my voice low. I recall an English teacher in grammar school who forced pupils to stand at the front of class and sing a song if they came last in the spelling test. He is the reason I can spell! I also remember him attempting to explain to the class that sentences could be long, illustrating with an example from a book he held up to the class, and announcing, "I know it because I wrote that sentence. I wrote the book." I was impressed. As a rule, the arts calmed me. I loved words and I loved pictures, so any subjects related to this were enjoyable. It was maths where I struggled, my final GCSE maths grade very much left wanting. A maths teacher in middle school even started to give me exam points for simply putting my name on the paper I was so bad. My interest in academics had slipped by the time I was in grammar school. I was no longer the studious high achiever I had been from the age of four through eleven. As my obsession ceased to be academics and instead became boys, my school grades slipped at the same rate. My academic obsession did not reignite until I was twenty-four.

The acne plummeted my self-esteem further. I wore make-up in a bid to cover the spots, but it was ineffective. I remember reading one evening that neat TCP was the answer, so quickly grabbed some cotton wool, soaked it in the astringent and daubed it all over my face. The following day I woke to burnt skin, layers of which were peeling from my face. My skin had wrinkled like that of an elderly lady. I kept my head down all day and made excuses to questions as to why my skin looked so poorly. In today's world I would most likely have been to see a dermatologist and prescribed Accutane tablets. My eldest child Laura fortunately takes after her dad for her skin, she did not inherit the acne. Oliver is his dad's doppelgänger, so is pretty safe, but I am fairly sure my youngest Ben may be next in line. Ben has elevated levels of self-esteem; he is a confident little boy. I am hoping this will be his blessing in avoiding how I felt during my teenage years. I responded to my acne by quickly growing a long fringe, and pretty much hiding behind it for six years. My last significant spot went at age twenty-four, and they were mostly gone by my early twenties. I wouldn't wish it on any teenager, nor the jibes and comments that I received off the back of it. To this day, my make-up is still my mask. The only time I do not wear make-up is when I go running, solo, and when I am in bed. The upside of oily skin, of course, is that it serves you better in later years; it prevents wrinkles, and I have been lucky enough to have grown and birthed three children without stretchmarks. My greasy skin is like wearing permanent moisturiser, constantly secreting oil. The downside is I am constantly managing shine and need to wash my hair daily because that is greasy too. Appearance should not matter, but when you have something in your physical appearance that sets you apart from the majority population, it does matter. Let us not fool ourselves that we live in a society that does not measure its people by appearance. It is everywhere, and we all subscribe to it to a greater or lesser extent. It is a multi-billion-pound global industry, appearance does matter, and to many. My teenage appearance simply added to my sense of not belonging.

Given that Autism is a 'whole body' condition, it may come as no surprise that the fear and anxiety emerging at the age of three would not be my only challenge. Yes, anxiety is without doubt the single most problematic comorbidity I experience. It is relentless, and it sits in the background constantly. It is my monster, it is chained to me, and though it has to an extent been tamed, it is very much still there. I should be very clear in saying that we are not talking about the type of anxiety that helps us to perform, we are talking instead about an anxiety that has longevity beyond threat, which has lots of unpleasant symptoms and other comorbidities, and has an impact on me every single day. Many people confuse healthy anxiety, which is purposeful and a normal part of the human condition, with anxiety disorder. They are different. Performance anxiety is helpful, there to step us up to the mark, or to save our life. My anxiety is slowly killing me. The second comorbidity of my undiagnosed autism, which started to emerge in my teens, was gastric problems. It arrived subtly at first, the sense that I did not quite have full control over my bodily functions. Certain foods would trigger it, particularly high fibre foods, the healthy ones!

The acne, anxiety and gastric problems made my adolescence miserable. I felt sad, lonely and unlovable. I hated myself. I survived those years because the concept that human beings can choose to end a painful life had thankfully not yet entered my cognition. I wanted to be like my popular and pretty girlfriends who had mothers who were easy to live with, and a string of admiring males in their trail. I am an observer, I watched the subtle compliments, stolen glances across their way, the body language. I watched from the outside. Those girls could not even see it, or if they could, they were not acknowledging it. I tried hard to fit in, to be like them, and not to mess up socially. But trying too hard often meant that I did.

I had developed maternal and mothering instincts early on in my teens, though luckily my inability to ensnare Mr Right (they were all Mr Right) to requite my love ensured that I did not get pregnant yet. Had my love been requited,

I believe I would have been pregnant earlier in my teens. I went from being obsessed with a fellow pupil I will call 'Mr Out of Town' at the age of thirteen to 'Mr He-Lust-Rious' during my mid-teens, who kindly reminded me that he 'would never go out with me because I was a fucking ugly bitch', to 'Mr Take What's Not Yours', a typical older bad guy who syphoned petrol and engaged in other petty crime, plus a few more minor people obsessions in between. And they *were* obsessions – boys and men I felt should be with me and whom I believed would fulfil my every need. What bullshit I had told myself. I had watched so many romantic films, learned from the various Cinderellas what to expect, so much so that I believed wholeheartedly in fairy tales and happy endings. Romance was an all or nothing thing for me. Whether it was *Dirty Dancing*, *Salsa*, *Can't Buy Me Love*, or *Some Kind of Wonderful*, I had watched them all, and upwards of a hundred times each. I knew each script, I knew the beautiful warm emotions they elicited in me, and I wanted some of that for myself. There were no unhappy endings in the movies I watched – see for yourself, the films tell you that. My knight in shining armour was out there. And yes, he most certainly was, but it was never a man. It was finding my truth, finding me. Like many Autistic people, we learn from books and movies what to expect. We idealise romantic relationships. Of course, reality can never live up to these idyllic notions of romance and, following my break-up with my second husband, a friend said to me, "I think you actually need someone who will constantly worship you like a princess." Well, yes, isn't that what happened to Cinderella?! That is what I read, didn't you? All or nothing.

Given that I hated adolescence, the first opportunity I had to leave it behind I took. I left school in May 1989 at the age of fifteen and in June started working at a motor trade training centre in Armthorpe. I started out on a Youth Training Scheme, or YTS as they were called at the time, earning a grand total of £29.50 per week, and I spent every single penny, every single week. I still wasn't good with money. I managed to buy clothes, go out around town pretending to be neurotypical, and eat a few KFCs on that meagre income. It was in my first job that I met my now lifelong friend Sam, one of my few neurotypical female friends who has remained the duration. Sam is one of my friends who takes control and allows me to take a back seat yet still feel safe in doing so. I trust her. If we have a girly weekend away, Sam will prepare the itinerary and plans, always with a 'What do you fancy doing while we are there?' or 'Are you okay with that?' Never a fait accompli, but always the plan and the level of predictability that Autistic people need to feel safe. This very morning my friend Sam has texted me with a plan ahead of a trip we will take next month. If the plan is changed for any reason, I will sometimes forget the new plan due to my executive functioning issues, and it wouldn't be the first time we have ended up at two different locations for a meal out! I think Sam understands I am different, and I genuinely believe our friendship will grow old with us. My first employment was also the place where I met the final human obsession of my teens, and the man who was to become the father of my firstborn child, Laura.

My first partner and 'husband-to-be' was thirty-seven and I was seventeen, exactly twenty years and six months older, another relationship now explained and understood through my Autistic lens. Autistic people tend to connect better with those not in our own age group. My partner and I connected. He was a thirty-seven-year-old man who looked and acted younger than his years. He charmed and swept me off my feet with his humour, his stories and, on reflection, his greater life experience. I am ashamed to say he was married, unhappily at the time, but nevertheless married. But it was too late because he was my obsession. We were together six months when, after his separation, we decided to try to get pregnant. I was eighteen. It took another six months. Understandably, our families where not approving of our relationship, but my family reached acceptance soonest. My partner's family reached acceptance when, nine months later, they met our beautiful baby daughter, and my constant need to belong allowed me to forgive their late arrival to the party. Over the course of the pregnancy, I slowly moved in with my partner. I don't ever recall the day when I officially moved out from my parents' home, but instead a piece-by-piece shift towards my partner's home, and a prompt leap out of adolescence and into adulthood. Unconsciously, I had engineered the hallmarks of adulthood because I could not cope with adolescence. I had secured a full-time job, related admin qualifications – Business and Administration NVQs and all stages of RSA typing, including a touch-typing speed of around 70 wpm – and I now had a man (who I would marry in 1997), a beautiful baby, and I lived in my partner's home. Adolescence gone!

CHAPTER FOUR

In Sickness and in Health...
But Not in Mental Health!

I was now a mum, a mother, and I unconsciously believed 'motherhood' would be an identity that would allow me to finally 'fit in'. It did not. I took my little baby to weigh-in sessions at my local GP practice; none of the mums spoke to me. I dreaded going, I felt uncomfortable and outcasted. It was a long walk to the surgery, uphill with a bulky pram, and going out with my baby was scary. I was fearful of crossing the road, scared of people looking at me, simply scared of people. A well-intentioned but overbearing relative took over the control of every aspect of my motherhood, and I had no confidence left. Just like all the other times in my life where I would feel controlled by other people or other things, I felt suffocated, like I was slowly dying, but did not have the social skills to redress this. I spoke to my GP about how I felt, told him I thought I was depressed or may have post-natal depression, but he said not. Nothing I could do was good enough. Other mums chit-chatted together with their bundles of joy as I sat there feeling alone, always feeling like I could cry. The exclusion and discomfort would be a repeated pattern in the coming years.

When Laura started primary school, other mums would congregate in their close circles and cliques, reinforcing the belief that I was not likeable and did not belong, always on the outside looking in, but never a participant. Swim class and gym class just the same. I quickly learned that motherhood is not an automatic ticket to human connection. I blamed myself. I knew I came across as aloof, but knew I wasn't. That doesn't matter, though, if no one can get past the vibe I am giving off. Aloof in my case can be explained as the feeling that I do not want to force my company on you, I do not feel like I am worth it, or my voice is worth it. I feel uncomfortable and need people to make me feel safe to participate. My close friendships have all developed from my working life. They started as goal orientated mutually justifiable interactions, where self-worth wasn't a factor, all except one, my best friend Vicky. Vicky and I met at university. She was the person who, when the only person I connected with at university left the course after three months, said to me, "Come on, you can hang around with us!" Vicky took me under her wing and has never released me since. My small quality not quantity group of girlfriends are priceless, I love them all – Sam, Vicky, Donna, Pam and my cousin Karen.

It will come as no surprise that my relationship and subsequent marriage to my first husband at the age of twenty-one was short-lived. My decree absolute was received at the age of twenty-four, following an acrimonious custody battle, which stretched out to County Court, and a less important but challenging battle over financial assets, of which there were very few because neither of us had been working for a year during the relationship, and because we had expended more money than was coming in! Debts had to be cleared first, plus the mounting legal fees. Ultimately, there was only one winner, as is the case in most marital breakdowns that require the services of legal teams. I recall needing the services of a barrister at County Court. My solicitor informed me that the hourly rate would be £150 but if I paid the barrister £600, they would work for as long as it took that day. I paid the £600 and the matter was signed, sealed and delivered within an hour!

My marriage to my first husband was my first failed relationship, and for me just another hallmark of failure, which would now include divorcee and, later, twice divorcee. This would be the first of two failed marriages, and two weddings – crying on arrival at both, which I now recognise was due to overwhelm and fear of social gatherings. I have read, though I genuinely cannot remember where, that the divorce rate is supposedly 30% higher in Autistic people, although previous research on the divorce rate being higher amongst parents of children with Autism appears to have been debunked. If indeed it is higher amongst Autistics themselves, it is likely to be explained by the many additional challenges faced within our intimate relationships as well as in our other relationships. Effective relationships require effective communication, remember the triad of impairment?

I met my second husband in 1997 and we were dating by 1998. He was six years my senior, so another age gap, but significantly narrowed in comparison to marriage number one. I had met him at work, he was a colleague. When I first met him, I did not care for him. I found him aloof and antisocial. I knew at the time that he had been promoted, and now being my boss could potentially make life hard for me if I did not try to get on with him, so I did, and a little too well as it turned out. Over time, I saw another side to him, a more lovable side, though in the coming years I would start to recognise a person with whom I was losing connection. Unfortunately, I did not consciously acknowledge this at the time, to both our detriment. I never saw my husband angry with a passion, anything with a passion, but he *was* intellectual with a passion, and this I was attracted to. From the workplace psychometric tests he had undertaken, he was shown to be in the top 5% of the population when it came to intelligence. He was gifted. He had the fastest reading speed of anyone I knew, would consume books by the day, and if you got him talking about the bigger questions in life, he was both loquacious and mind blowing. Like myself at the time, he was working in logistics, but his gift would have been put to such greater benefit as a writer or academic, much like his own father. My second husband was aware of this, but like so many adults, recognised his need to earn a living and felt he could best meet that need in his current occupation rather than following a less secure dream. His steadfast commitment to logistics has been a loss to academia, but the transport industry's gain. I also benefited from that commitment, which allowed me to reduce my working hours to undertake an undergraduate degree between 2003-2006.

Following my graduation in 2006, my second husband and I discussed having a baby. We had Laura, of course, whom my husband was raising as his stepdaughter, though Laura did not always make it easy for him, for reasons which hereto will be explained. My husband was reluctant with the idea of more children, but continued to engage in discussions, led largely by me. Ultimately, the truth was he did not want children, his own, or anyone else's for that matter. We simply wanted different things in life, and that is okay, but I really wish we had discussed this earlier in the relationship, not eight years in! At that point, it was too late. Through persuasion, my husband was willing to try for a baby, but I always sensed it was not for him. I was in denial. A year in, we were still not pregnant and decided, again with persuasion on my part, to visit the local fertility clinic. The clinical conclusion of those visits was that we were unlikely to conceive without clinical intervention in the form of IVF. My husband point blank refused this, with logical and intellectual reasoning, to which I concurred. Instead, he was willing to explore adoption.

We started the application to adopt and took part in the subsequent interview processes with the social workers. However, on my birthday in November 2008, I was contacted at work to be told the team would not be pursuing our application further on the grounds that they did not believe my husband wanted more children, and the secondary belief that I still wanted more biological children. They had done their job exceptionally well and I am now incredibly grateful for that, mostly for the sake of an unadopted child who would go on to a family who genuinely wanted them in their lives. Our relationship plummeted at that point, with crisis talks on the 19th of December 2008 and our consequent split in February 2009, incidentally the same month I split with my first husband, not the most romantic of months for me!

I fought ferociously to prevent my husband leaving, but in hindsight I now know the split was right for us both. My second husband is today married to the ex-wife of a couple we had been close friends with during our relationship together. These couple friends we had shared weekends away with, many a New Year's Eve, including the millennium, and were friends with whom my second husband was already acquainted before I met him. As it turned out, they were *his* friends, not mine. I would soon find out that this was the case with most of our so-called friends. They disappeared from my life nearly as fast as my husband. This was a life lesson to me, to always invest in your *own* friendships, not just those of your partner or who become couple-friends with you and your partner. If you ever break up, one of you will lose them. Whilst you might be thinking, is this chick stupid or what, her husband must have been having an affair before the split!? I do not believe my second husband and our friend's wife were having a relationship before we broke up. Their relationship was purely platonic. During a visit to discuss practical matters associated with the separation, which turned into a snot and tears performance from me, I asked my second husband, "Were you seeing her before we split?" he paused to think, looked me in the eye and said a drawn out, "Nooo." The pause, tone and timing were always questionable, and some might take this in such context to mean that what came next was a lie. I had always questioned the response, but I also knew my husband could not lie. On reflection, I later realised I had failed to seek the fullest truth by my ineffective questioning. My second husband answered the question literally. Had I added, "But did you *want* to?" in my opinion, the answer would have been yes, and that mattered. My second husband had paused to work out how he could answer my question without lying, and without escalating a situation that was already upsetting and volatile. He too did not like conflict, so he used the question literally to circumvent problems. He was smarter than me, but very few people reflect and over-analyse interaction as much as I do. I just needed time to work it out. This is the story of my life, people withholding truth in calculated ways, me always the last to switch on or get the joke, but with processing time, I get there in the end.

During the early part of our relationship, neither my second husband nor I had significant knowledge and understanding of mental ill health. My husband was aware that I experienced anxiety, and those around me were aware of the gastric problems I experienced, but none of us would have related these to undiagnosed autism. My husband seemed to be aware of the occasions when depression had crept in, at which point my low physical functioning rendered me unable to get out bed. I now view this as 'Autistic Burnout' rather than depression as the symptoms are quite similar and include extreme fatigue. On these occasions, my husband would take Laura out for the day and leave me alone. He was good at sensing my need. I suspect this helped him too because I think he simply did not know what to do with me.

My second husband worked long hours. He would leave work late, and then stop in at the local pub on the way home. He needed solitude as much as I did. He would arrive home any time between 7-8pm. We did not see a lot of him during the week and I often felt like a lone parent raising Laura. Both my first and second husbands' need to be anywhere other than with us, and with anyone other than with us, left me feeling lonely, sad and guilty for Laura. Even a neighbour said to me they thought I was lonely; I knew they felt sorry for me. I felt unloved and could not authentically reciprocate love because I did not love myself. When a person illustrates they do not want to be with you, it can easily affirm what you have always known; you are not worthy and not someone people want to be with. Feeling lonely in a relationship is the worst kind of loneliness. You are not set free; you are trapped. The contradiction... I would not set *myself* free because I was too scared of being alone! I knew deep down that being alone for the right reasons was better than being with someone for the wrong ones, but as usual I could not deliver. Living with someone who has ongoing and relentless mental health difficulties is not easy for anyone, it simply manifests 'in sickness and in health, but not in mental health'. My undiagnosed autism and related mental ill health came between us just as much as anything or anyone else.

My need for order and control was highly present throughout the eleven-year relationship. I had routines, just like Mum, cleaning Friday evening, top to bottom, exercise regimes, and my husband had to fit in and around that. I was being the unmasked me who has a need to be clean, tidy and organised – The Umbrella Picker. My husband used to call me 'Sue' in reference to my mum's name when he was irritated by this. This hurt me the most because I was trying so desperately *not* to become Mum. At the time, Mum's routines represented rejection, so the last thing I wanted was to be labelled 'Sue'. I believed that, because we were married, my husband had to stay with me no matter what. Today I know that people *choose* to stay with you and can also choose to leave. I take nothing for granted.

When personal relationships break down, I often find the held back opinion of others starts to emerge. Friends and family were more willing to tell me what they really thought of my ex-husband now that he was just that. Their thoughts aligned with those of my own initial thoughts – antisocial and aloof.

Though I am neither of their friends today, I carry no hatred or ill wishes for either of my ex-husbands, and I cannot shoulder responsibility for other people's thoughts and opinions of them. Hatred is, after all, neither good for man nor beast, and I am unwilling to carry a burden of hate. I hope my ex-husbands are both happy in their relationships and with life generally. Hey, who knows, if they happen across my book the connections may slot together for them too. Everyone needs closure, don't they? They too shared my journey of mental ill health and undiagnosed autism, but none of us knew that at the time and it now explains so much for us all.

CHAPTER FIVE

My Third Time Lucky

Following my split with my second husband, I put any ideas of love, romance and babies to the very recesses of my mind. I had accepted myself as single and it felt good. It was also a first for me since my teenage years.

I was working within the NHS at the time, managing a workplace mental health project, a move into a field of work in which I was *extremely interested*, and a move that would turn out to be the second place of searching for my true identity, the first being my degree in criminology and years spent studying crime. Some might even say I searched in 'bad' and I searched in 'mad'. I would not use the latter term because I know just how stigmatising language like that can be for people who experience mental health difficulties, myself included. But indeed, I searched for a long time in both, and to an extensive level.

The NHS project was a temporary one, a three-year fixed-term contract, and one that I was halfway through at the time my husband and I split. I was aware of the vulnerability of my single parent income and looming contract end date. I squirreled money aside, Laura and I living quite frugally. My inability to manage money had been reformed at the age of twenty-seven when the anxiety of not having money for unforeseeable circumstances and 'rainy days' became more challenging than that of saving. Is this not usually the case? We change when the pain of staying the same exceeds the pain of change. Or, as I like to put it these days… Choose your pain – saving is hard, being in debt is hard! The balance had been tipped towards the desired behaviour. I was fortunate that Laura and I did not lose our home during this time; we would have had nowhere to go. My second husband continued to contribute to the mortgage payments to ensure we had a home. This I was exceptionally grateful for. I was also confident he did not want the negative impact of missed mortgage payments or repossession on his financial record, though I knew the support would only be short-lived, and I'd had to agree to put the house on the market.

Mum and Dad would not take Laura and I in, they had refused after my first marriage break-up, and they were in no position to financially assist. I had no safety net after any of my marriage breakdowns due to Mum's undiagnosed autism and inability to cope with change. Her routines could not be challenged by unplanned guests. I mistakenly thought everyone could go back home when they were on their arse and the chips were down, but for me it was different. For a long time, I felt let down by my parents. I had no one to help me, financially or otherwise, and it led to the belief that I must rely solely on myself for my survival. Mum was of the 'you made your bed now lie in it' generation, and Dad followed suit. After my break-up with my first husband, I flat shared with a work colleague on and off, and I had to leave Laura in her dad's care and fight through the courts for this to be shared. This broke my heart into a thousand pieces. My case was successful, but I never felt like I had won. I felt empty. Today I recognise how close I came to homelessness. They always say you are only a few steps away from homelessness, or a few pay cheques. This was true for me and is one of the very reasons for my ongoing hard work and independence. No one will rescue me; I must save myself.

Laura was now an adolescent and goodness did I know it! She had not dealt well with the split between my second husband and I, and she was angry. This anger presented as lashing out verbally and physically and made life that bit harder. She was now in high school and experiencing many of the challenges that I had encountered during my own teenage years, less the acne, her father's genetics to be thankful for. But she did not fit in.

Laura started to identify with the 'emo' sub-culture, fitting the classic stereotype both emotionally and aesthetically. She dyed her hair from blonde to black and moved in and amongst those of her own kind. She was more independent now and spent time outdoors with her small group of friends, some of whom remain her close friends today. Her challenging behaviour at home led to me eventually contacting school and social services for additional support, and so we entered the Common Assessment Framework (CAF) to establish unmet needs and access additional support from the social system.

Regular 'Team Around the Child' (TAC) meetings took place, attended by those who had a professional and personal interest in Laura's well-being. The fathers and father figures in Laura's life rarely if ever attended. Today Laura regularly sees her biological father, but has seen my second husband only once since our split in 2009. There is no contact with him today.

Notwithstanding raising a troubled teenager, I had settled into a period of being comfortable alone, albeit with fears around financial vulnerability and the near end date to my employment contract. It was at this time that I was introduced to two new relationships that would shape and alter my life's direction forever...

When you go through life's biggest challenges, there's always that friend who walks with you through the pain as if it's theirs too, the friend you can rely on, the friend you can send angry text messages as damage limitation to stop you sending them directly to your ex. That friend was Pam. She walked through the quagmire with me, and as it turns out, she was also the person to introduce me to my now-husband Steven. She walked with me through the dark then pointed me in the direction of light...

"He says you're a MILF!"

"Give over! He's only blooming twelve!" (To be clear, I was exaggerating!)

"He isn't! He's twenty-one."

"Well, that's still too young. I'm thirty-four."

Despite my reservations and protestations, I agreed to a date with Steven at Pam's house, a BBQ. Hey, what would be the harm in a bit of 'fun'? I was free, single and old enough to make choices like this. And besides, I had not had any 'fun' during my adolescence. I had been a mum since nineteen! Was this not now my time? Following my break-up with my second husband, I had questioned whether I knew how to love, or to love properly, so maybe 'fun' was safer for someone like me. What I did not appreciate is that Jane McNeice does not do fun, she does serious, overly serious. She does, in fact, love. I recognise it today in that if I were to lose what I care most deeply about, my husband and children, it would rip a gaping hole in my heart. That hole would sit alongside a hole that formed in 2014 when I lost my brother. I do love, but like most things, the cognitive part of love for me is probably wired a bit differently to others. I am also someone who cannot mask love, I cannot fake it, nor can I give dishonest compliments or feedback. If you are ever on the receiving end of love, care, or feedback from me, you can be assured it is always honest, despite the dishonesty contained within my masks, which I will talk about more in chapter eight. However, I do want to be clear in saying the intention of my masks is only ever to fit in, not to be dishonest, but I am acutely aware of their inevitable deceit.

Anyway, where was I with the MILF story? This is a perfect example of my self-titled 'brain firework' where my Autistic brain goes off on a tangent, and I have to reign it in. You'll see it throughout the book. I'm trying so hard to keep on topic! … So, 'fun' happened for a few months, but behind the fun both of us wanted more, we wanted the serious. The hooks were already in on both sides. Pam knew this, but Steven and I were in denial, until of course Pam pointed it out to both of us. So, we stopped, we talked, and we went back to the start. We had a bona fide date night, dressed up, and our first meal (BBQ notwithstanding) was at an Italian restaurant in Sheffield. Things were going well, but over the Christmas of that year, I had experienced a relapse in my mental health, depression had once more crept in, caused in the main by work-related stress.

When you attribute the breakdown of your last relationship to your mental ill health, you do not let rejection grace your door twice. I immediately pushed Steven away, thinking he would run for the hills anyway, so I took control first. He resisted, he did not run, he stayed. As it turned out, Steven *could* and *can* support mental ill health. He supported me, he listened. Steven is thirteen years my junior, and again our connection can likely now be explained through my Autism and the greater affinity Autistic people experience with those not of our own age. That said, when you marry a man old enough to be your father, then one nearly young enough to be your son, you inevitably question, am I normal? You question it because big age gap relationships are not considered 'normal' or the neurotypical ideal; you are still measuring yourself against neurotypical. The simple answer is: no, I am not 'normal', I am not neurotypical, I am neurodivergent. I am 'normal' for an Autistic person, or, at the very least, for this Autistic person, because we are all different. You must surely now be thinking, seriously, how the hell *was* she missed!?

Our relationship developed and Steven and I decided to move in together. Though Steven has always respected my need for space and a level of solitude, we live together with ease. We rarely argue, and if we do, it is always about food and usually when my husband is hangry (angry because you are hungry)! Laura got on well with Steven, and to this day, still gets on well with him. I never placed any responsibility on Steven to be anything to Laura, not to be a father, just to be kind to her. As it turned out, he has been the best dad she could ask for. He has experienced her ups and downs and dealt with things an older man would have run a mile from. He has felt her pain just the same as I have.

Eventually, Steven and I had to sever the financial ties still remaining with my second husband. Steven sold one of his beloved cars, a BMW Z4, the first of what would be his many car loves and bought in to our mortgage and house, which was at the time in negative equity on the back of the recession. It doesn't sound an attractive deal, does it?!

At the right time, the topic of babies emerged. Steven had said that he did not want children until his thirties, and I had joked that they would not be with me then. I would be in my forties! So, for anyone thinking there may have been a baby-making ulterior motive in my relationship with a younger man, it was most definitely the last thing on my mind. My baby dreams had long since been put to bed. But that all changed when, in a surprising U-turn, Steven one day said, "Would you like to have a baby? I love you and I'd love to have a baby with you." Wow, I did not expect that! And a little spark of a flame that I thought had fizzled out reignited inside. We *both* wanted a baby, and that baby would be made with love, and loved by both of us in equal measure.

In a story of history repeating, our pregnancy attempts failed over the next eighteen months and once again I found myself under the auspices of the local fertility clinic. Twice in any lifetime sounds unfortunate, but I am not unfortunate, and I am not unlucky. On both occasions the universe was at play, serving what I now believe was the right thing at the right time. But, without wanting to sound *too* fatalistic, I know the true reason we were not conceiving was biological; it was the level of stress I experienced, and my inability to manage it. I believe Autism played its part hereto. I know this because the clinical outcome on this occasion was 'unexplained infertility' couched as 'nothing wrong, it's just not happening, and we don't know why'. I had blood tests, invasive examinations, and a fibroid removed from my uterus, a fibroid that turned out *not* to be a fibroid, just an irregularity. For couples with unexpected infertility, the offering ahead of IVF is IUI (intrauterine insemination) – where fertility doctors put the sperm right next to the egg and say 'Hey, look here little sperm, there's the egg, now swim!' This procedure is less invasive and cheaper than IVF. As we already had a child, we could not access the financial support of the NHS. However, before IUI we were invited to try fertility drugs as a first intervention. Fertility drugs come with a risk of multiple gestation – lots of babies! Careful what you wish for! Today with my current level of professional understanding, I fully recognise the role that stress played and just how damaging it is to the human body, both mentally and physically. My body was unwilling to grow another person until I could prioritise myself and prove I was doing so; further testimony that self-care comes first. Even mother nature tells us in her own little way!

My yearning for a second child had been long-standing and emotionally painful. Is it not always the case that when you want to get pregnant, and especially when it is not happening for you, in everyone else it seems to be – pregnancy and baby announcements are everywhere! Planned ones, it accidentally happened ones, our little surprise ones, the latter even *more* soul-destroying. You try so hard to be pleased for others, to double the amount of joy by sharing and being part of theirs, but instead it feels like a knife through the heart and through the uterus at the same time. I could not bury my hurt. What you see is what you get when I meltdown, which is when my presentation is most honest. To this day, I have watched others lie with a poker face so convincing that I am in awe. This could be explained by the fact that Autistic people cannot lie, and if we try, we fail miserably. Neurotypicals are much more adept at this than us. Come on, you've all done it. Ever tell someone you were fine when really you weren't? Of course you have. My face immediately gives away how I feel, even though I mask. Despite being Autistic, or perhaps *because* I am Autistic, when I have set my sights on life's goals, I have achieved them. I have taken control, put in the hard work, and made it happen. For the first time, I could not make this happen, no amount of control or effort could make us pregnant, and the most difficult emotion I experienced was frustration.

Until around three years ago, I experienced what I call pregnancy envy, an intense jealousy at seeing other pregnant women. I continued to have the emotional memory and mindset of a woman who could not get pregnant, so I have a great deal of empathy for those who cannot and cherished my own later fertility. Now, after having had three children and nearing my forty-sixth birthday, I take preventative measures in the form of the contraceptive pill, but I have never been able to conquer the next step and fully end my fertility years through intervention. This would be the right choice now, especially because my executive functioning means I can sometimes forget to take my pill! My practice nurse recently bantered, "Come on, Jane, you are not fifteen now."

On the back of my diagnosis, however, my mindset has shifted. I am now fine, I am done with any issue I had around prized fertility, no longer experience pregnancy envy, and the next time I visit the nurse for my pill check, I will be discussing what they seem to call 'having your tubes tied', which is always interesting for someone who thinks in pictures! My infertility story is also karma, since my first husband and his ex-wife could not have children. That was a major source of their own relationship breakdown, and my ending up with him. I cannot begin to imagine how much she may have hated me when I was pregnant with her ex-husband's first child, and for this I am terribly sorry. Karma has everyone's address, and my own fertility challenges years later was my likely payback. I know the disappointment of knowing that your period has started when you thought you might be pregnant, when intimate relations become overshadowed by thoughts of whether this time will be *the* time you conceive. It's sickening and it is painful.

During this period of unsuccessful fertility, Steven and I were dealt one of the biggest challenges of our relationship to date. I was driving home one Friday night full of the Friday feeling and listening to 'Wherever You Will Go' by The Calling, a song that still brings those cognitive and emotional memories flooding back even today. Steven called me while I was on the motorway and said, "I think Laura is pregnant." Silence.

I arrived home to a letter from Laura, the most eloquent and heartfelt piece she has ever written, telling me she was pregnant. I could not deal with the truth, the truth that my fifteen-year-old daughter was having a baby. I said she had to go and live with her dad, and if she wanted to come home then she must terminate the pregnancy. Despite the shock, I had already predicted this teenage pregnancy would happen, and a friend quickly reminded me of this when I told her the news. This is just one of my 'fortune-telling' pattern-spotting predictions made years earlier that I am sure some readers will feel could so easily have been self-fulfilling prophecy, and they could be right. Maybe there *was* a vibe I had given off, maybe it was down to my own desperate need to have another baby that advertised just how wonderful being a mum is. Nevertheless, I had seen it coming when Laura was just a child. She *was* still a child, wasn't that the point!?

Knowing in my heart of hearts the risk that my child would get pregnant in her teens, I had always encouraged her to dream big, talked to her about going to university, the benefits of having a career and travelling to the destinations of her dreams *before* settling down. I knew that one of the best ways to deter teenage pregnancy was to instil ambition in young girls, not to make motherhood the default position for girls and women. I tried desperately to instil a different dream in Laura.

My initial response to Laura's announcement had come from the head, but a few days later, my heart re-engaged, and I was able to say, "I will support you in whatever decision you take." Steven struggled with the news; he talked about leaving. I took the difficult decision that first and foremost my daughter needed me, and I had to support her, and Steven needed to do whatever was right for him. Steven decided to stand by us too, and our relationship went from strength-to-strength. The relationship between Laura and me also improved, which I believe was due to the final recognition on Laura's part that I would do *anything* for her, and she was loved.

You would think that as a woman desperate to become pregnant, now with her fifteen-year-old daughter with child, that it would be like an arrow to the heart watching her swollen tummy grow. It was quite the opposite, it provided a healing to my own need, to have a baby in our world that was a part of my daughter and therefore a part of me. No, it was not the dream I had for Laura, but a dream was surely unfolding and coming true. I reminded Laura that the other dreams could still happen but would now happen in a different order to that anticipated. I am also mindful that they may have been my dreams and never Laura's.

Evie Rose was born in January 2012, and she really was a rosebud. She filled a space in our hearts that we did not even know was missing. The small family unit that we were at the time allowed us to play a significant role in Laura and Evie's life, and it also took away the pressures of our own failing pregnancy attempts. We simply got on with life as it was. We planned to travel, something that we were already enjoying, having just had a holiday together in the Maldives, our favourite place in the world to this day, and a place we have been lucky enough to revisit.

Stress and anxiety were still a significant feature of my everyday life, and the reason we were not conceiving, but in October 2012 I had an unusual couple of weeks of harmonious bliss. I had been looking forward to an arts and crafts retreat I was due to attend, making stained glass ornaments. I cared less about the day-to-day stressors. The fertility drugs had just run out, and I joked with a colleague, "I bet it happens now." By the time I attended the retreat I was pregnant.

Life then happened very quickly. Our house had been stagnant on the housing market since my split with my second husband nearly four years earlier and both Steven and I wanted to live in a home we chose together. This being the case, we had simply left the property for sale, with no great urgency and no price reduction. Three years, one grandchild and another baby on the way, people became interested in our property, lots of people. We sold and moved out of the property and into the home we live in today in June 2013, only exchanging contracts on completion day, all of our furniture sitting in a 7.5 tonne lorry on the drive – our baby was due in four days! Had it fallen through on completion day, we would have needed to unpack the lorry and take two steps back with a baby on the way. We were like a TV mortgage advert balanced on a knife edge.

Mother nature had played her card once more and my body managed to keep our baby warm and snug until the last box was unpacked on a sunny afternoon early in July. The following morning, nine days after his due date, our first baby boy arrived, the baby I had waited an awfully long time for. We were bursting with love. Oliver James was the easiest of my three births, number two of three. More about our youngest later.

When I had Laura at the young age of nineteen, I had a birth experience very much the product of its time – episiotomy as standard, stitching back together, opiates for the pain and an epidural to ensure you have very little control over your birth. One birth like that is enough for any lifetime! This time I took control. After staying at home from my first contraction at around 3am, until around 7.40am when we got in the car, I hypnobirthed my baby out at the local hospital at 8.55am with a simple TENS machine for assistance. I was home the following day and could have done it all again the day after! We would have been home the same day had it not been for the fact that Oliver had done a motion on the way out and the nursing team wanted to be sure he hadn't swallowed any.

My second child was a long time coming – an eighteen-year gap between Laura and Oliver – to the point I had accepted more children was not going to be. Even during the pregnancy, I experienced waves of disbelief that there was going to be another child and spent the first year after Oliver's birth pinching myself that my dreams had come true. Oliver was a spindly, thin-limbed little baby, with big brown eyes and the most kissable cherry lips you could imagine. Today these remain his finest features. He is his father's doppelgänger in all except one feature, his blond hair, courtesy of me.

Laura was still living at home with Evie, now with myself, Steven and her baby brother Oliver. Laura remained with us for another two years until her second pregnancy when she and her partner, her now-husband Alex, moved into a home of their own. To this day, Oliver and Evie remain close, and despite the age gap, Laura and Oliver still have the type of sibling repartee where Laura can tease and mock her brother, but if anyone else was to do this she would intervene like only a sibling can. Once upon a time, Oliver was teeny weeny next to the taller Evie, but Evie is pocket-sized, a Kylie Minogue in the making, and he is now at least two head sizes above her.

I had always told Steven that I would never marry for a third time, despite the fact I loved him dearly, and our child Oliver. So, when Steven crouched down one Spring evening in 2015 and asked me to marry him, I was as surprised by my own response as much as the proposal. I said yes, he is my third time lucky. I told you I wasn't unlucky!

Neither of us wanted a staged and prescribed 'big day'. I had, in fact, already done that and still felt the negative impact of the idea of two failed marriages, plus I had heard so many judgemental comments over the years about those on their *third* marriage. Like we are marriage pariahs, faulty goods. So, we chose instead to adapt an already booked holiday to the Seychelles and added the 'wedding package' to this.

On 30th September 2015, Oliver, now eighteen months old, held up a placard on the beach inscribed, "My mummy and daddy got married in secret today, but I don't know what a secret is…" We posted a photo of this on social media to announce our news to friends and family and sent bespoke postcards from the Seychelles inviting everyone to a post-wedding get-together. To the well-trained eye, my Autistic traits could even be seen on our wedding day. I fluffed my marriage lines due to my social communication difficulties and the photographer had me close my eyes between photos, so that I could open them without squinting for the pictures. I cannot open my eyes in bright sunlight without sunglasses. 'Sunglass wearing wedding dress' was not the look I was going for that day! Hypersensitivity (or hyposensitivity) to light (and/or noise, temperature, touch, etc.) is one of the many sensory challenges experienced by Autistic people. The world is a much visually brighter place for some of us, a bit like turning the brightness up on your phone or tablet. During the summer months, I pretty much live in my shades. My late brother was the same. Sensory challenges aside, our wedding day ultimately remained about the most important thing, our love. As I write today, we have just shared our sixth wedding anniversary and our twelfth year together. Never underestimate the power of 'fun' to connect you forever.

CHAPTER SIX

Mind Matters,
It Was No Coincidence

So how does an undiagnosed Autistic woman end up working in mental health, doing a job that, on paper, she should not be able to do successfully? Because she is determined, and she is still searching, of course, *and* because she feels other people's pain as if it is her own.

She has already searched for herself in the criminal fraternity, and now she is looking for herself in those with mental health problems. She has spent a lifetime self-analysing, so understanding the mind is not something unfamiliar to her. She also refers to herself in the third person, and she does this because she experiences a diffuse sense of self, often seen in Autistic people, and which can also be present in mental health conditions such as Bipolar Disorder, Emotionally Unstable Personality Disorder (sometimes referred to as borderline personality disorder) and trauma-related diagnosis. This is one of several explanations for misdiagnosis of these mental health conditions in undiagnosed autistic people before the truth is found. That said, it *is* possible to have both Autism and other mental health diagnoses, and, of course, possible to have mental health diagnoses and not have Autism, but there are *definite* patterns of misdiagnosis. **Only** can a ***well-informed and acutely mental health and autism aware*** **clinically qualified professional** make the most accurate judgement on all counts. I make no apologies for the bold emphasis here. Letters before or after your name are not enough, and they offer no guarantee of accuracy, as my own story attests.

Setting up my company Mind Matters, and the preceding journey into the field of mental health, were no accident. Both were unconsciously engineered for reasons related to undiagnosed autism, and only on reflection is this so blindingly obvious to me. My workplace is a safe place to be. I work alongside my daughter, so neither of us needs to socially mask with one another. I only mask when I am delivering training, which is just part of the time.

I had, by this point, already been given or worked out other identities for myself. I was clinically diagnosed as having GAD (Generalised Anxiety Disorder) and irritable bowel syndrome. I was the rare Myers Briggs Type Indicator[15] 'INFJ' (introverted, intuitive, feeling, judging), which I'd now translate as ~~introverted~~ meltdown avoidant, ~~intuitive~~ pattern-spotting, ~~feeling~~ empath and ~~judging~~ honest. I was a 'left-brain thinker' with a dominant left-brain, though today I am illustrated to be a mix of both left and right – I was curious to see which way the ballerina was spinning for me today, so I just rechecked it and I can switch between clockwise and anti-clockwise and show as left and right-brain on other tests too. If the talk of ballerinas has you thinking 'where on earth has she gone now?! Is this another 'brain firework'?' Let me explain! The spinning ballerina is an online video showing a silhouetted spinning ballerina. According to the research, whether you interpret the ballerina as spinning clockwise or anti-clockwise should indicate whether you are left or right-brain dominant. Go ahead, satisfy your curiosity, you won't get the few minutes back, but it's insightful https://www.youtube.com/watch?v=2RSsoTJA6cA

According to Belbin's Team Role Inventory[16] I am a 'Completer-Finisher', so I get things done, a typical Autistic trait, and according to Neil Fleming's VARK (Visual, Auditory, Reading/Writing, Kinaesthetic)[17] model, my learning preference is that of 'Visual Learner', no surprises there! According to Honey and Mumford's Learning Style[18] model of Activist, Pragmatist, Theorist and Reflector, I am a Theorist, but score very closely behind as a Reflector. The fact that I have, over the years, put myself into all these various boxes is not just down to the fact that I undertook CIPD (Chartered Institute of Personnel and Development) qualifications after my undergraduate degree, it is testimony to obsessive searching and a belief that if I could just find the right box, I would somehow *know* who I was. For years, my Associate Trainer Gemma, who is also my daughter's best friend from childhood, would say, "You've always needed a box, maybe there isn't a box for everyone." There was, I just hadn't found it yet.

My search in crime had, *fortunately* for me, not revealed a box or reflective identity, but I could not rule out that my mind was not unwell. After all, I was anxious all the time, there had to be something more to this.

My anxiety was emotionally painful, relentless and difficult to manage. When you wake up every single day of your life feeling frightened, you often wish you did not wake up at all. I will never in this lifetime know the feeling of waking up anxiety free. I live in a future that has not yet happened, I try to predict and control that future because everything about it frightens me. As previously mentioned, there are only three things in my life that provide cessation to that fear: 1) reading 2) writing and 3) sleep. I do not have a lot of sleep these days, but I do spend a great deal of my waking time reading and writing. The reading is one of the reasons I do not get enough sleep. The mantra on my headstone will one day be 'Just one more chapter…' A 'brain firework' has just gone off and my Autistic brain is now thinking of every other possibility I might want on my headstone and is completely contradicting my previous statement! My brain is constantly overthinking everything, until I go to sleep. Every single day I go to war on my fears and anxiety. Maybe now my task is to make peace with it, as I know it isn't going away. Living every day of your life with anxiety builds empathy for others who suffer similar issues. You know their pain. Which is why one of the most insulting and ill-founded myths I encounter as an Autistic person is the belief that we lack or do not have empathy. We do not feel. *The* most offensive belief I have ever read about autism is that we are dead souls in living bodies. It broke me. Not least because I believe in soul transition and spiritualism.

If you are to truly understand empathy, there are some critical things you need to know. Empathy comprises two elements, cognitive empathy and affective empathy, a bit like the memory recall. Cognitive empathy requires 'Theory of Mind', a cognitive mechanism identified by Autism researcher Simon Baron-Cohen, illustrated in his 'Sally-Ann Test', and something that many Autistic people have difficulty with. Theory of Mind is the ability to predict what others are thinking, their desires, emotions, intentions and suchlike. My own Theory of Mind tends to operate in reverse. Overall, I am a particularly good predictor of other people's thoughts and behaviours; they link to my behavioural-focused pattern-spotting. For me, the Theory of Mind difficulty presents as me thinking you should know what *I* am thinking, so I tend not to express how I feel, or ask for help. Sometimes I do not have the words, also known as Alexithymia, an inability to describe my emotions. I cannot verbally tell you how I feel, but I am better at doing so on paper. I generally assume you should already know. Your knowing would in fact give *me* insight at times! My husband falls foul of this when I expect that he should know if I am upset, so when his support is not forthcoming, I then feel hurt and dejected. I expect him to mind-read! So, because Autistic people lack Theory of Mind[19], otherwise known as mind-blindness, we are late to the party when it comes to '*cognitive* empathy'. *But*, when we arrive, we arrive *big* style, we are in no way lacking in '*affective* empathy'. We feel empathy at an amplified level, tenfold the level of most neurotypicals. We are, in some cases, super empaths – you cry, I taste your tears! When you feel other people's pain on such a level, you devote your life's purpose to removing and reducing suffering in whatever way you can. It is probably not as truly altruistic as that sounds, as it is about reducing it for ourselves too. Nevertheless, the mission of my business is to reduce the suffering caused by mental ill health, and I choose to do that by raising mental health literacy and equipping people with the skills, knowledge and confidence to support themselves and others who may be suffering. It is no accident that I ended up in the occupational field of mental health, or in a 'helping' profession.

On the topic of empathy, the National Autistic Society today cite several theorists who have explored what is called the 'Theory of Double Empathy'[20] or simply referred to as the double empathy problem. The basic thinking is that there is a lack of empathy just the same in Allistic (non-Autistic) people as there is claimed about Autistics, one does not empathise with the other, and in fact this is often the case in any group of people who have vastly different experiences of the world. There is no less empathy on one side that does not also exist on the other side too – the double empathy problem!

As part of my return to academia at the age of twenty-four, I started to study the mind, undertaking an A level psychology evening class and ~~coercing~~ persuading one of my best friends Donna to join me and 'mother' me through it. Donna, an archaeology graduate, had more recently left academia, and being the learned soul that she is, was easily ~~coerced~~ persuaded. One of the most intelligent and thought-provoking people I know, Donna strolled out of the course twelve months later with an A, nothing less than she is capable of. I fought studiously for twelve months and came out dragging my heels with a B, a less than predictable exam dropping my total grade from an A. My study of psychology continued, solo, in the form of an Access to Higher Education Social Sciences & Humanities course, and further psychological study during my undergraduate degree, though my occupation at the time remained in logistics.

As part of the practical arrangements needed to fulfil my academic studies, I now had to take part-time work rather than the full-time job I had. I also felt it would be healthier for me and my second husband, whom I had met while working in logistics, not to be working together and that it was time for me to move on. Though I did not take favourably to it initially, I took a job within the voluntary and community sector, working at a 'Voluntary Action' charity, a voluntary and community sector infrastructure organisation whose reason for being was to support local non-profits to do what they do best. Shifting from the private sector to the third sector was a shock to the system that felt like stepping back in time. In time, I would come to love working for the charity, my most preferred employer and sector to date. I was Personal Assistant to the Chief Executive and remained so for the next five years. Following my graduation, I was able to secure a role within the same organisation as a Human Resources

& Business Advisor to the local third sector, but I never *truly* felt fulfilled in this role. HR wasn't really an area that interested me, yet I believed in the values of justice and fairness weaved through both it and the legislature, which I had also studied at A level and again during my undergraduate degree. Fairness and justice rank highly in the virtues of many Autistic people and are something we are often enthusiastic about. I cannot abide prejudice, inequality and discrimination, though my fear of conflict means I do not call it out enough when I see it. I then feel guilty, ashamed and become angry at my pathetic self for my weakness. I also internalise other people's complaints that too many of us do not call out prejudice and racism, but maybe it's easier to call such things out when you are neurotypical. If you are Autistic like me and conflict causes you to feel suicidal, then you must first weigh up a cost benefit that others cannot even begin to comprehend. It's easy to say call it out when you are assertive and confident.

Working for Voluntary Action Barnsley (now titled Barnsley CVS) put me in a position to acquire the vital skills that would help me to set up and run the company I own today. I quite literally spent the whole eight years blending in, listening, observing and soaking up knowledge like a sponge.

During the early part of my VAB career, my gastric problems were at their worst. I live with a bowel that I can only describe to others as fast, a bowel that I never quite feel in control of. These were the symptoms that started to emerge during adolescence. I am sure every reader can relate to this lack of control at some time or other. The problem was that now it was causing me constant distress and panic, especially in group situations and meetings where the control was even more difficult to maintain. Despite not feeling able to breathe, I masked the panic attacks. The panic was made worse if I was asked to speak in those meetings, at which point I just wanted to die. It was awful. My gastric problems were clinically diagnosed as irritable bowel syndrome, and various interventions were offered to no avail. Like a tormenting vicious circle, the gastric problems fed my anxiety, and my anxiety fed the gastric problems.

Following my graduation in 2006, I started exercising four or five days a week at the new local health club. I had spent nearly six years sitting on my bottom reading and drafting essays and my bottom now reflected the lack of physical activity. The exercise did not really help with the gastric problems, and the fear continued as well, but I did lose weight. I had by this time been diagnosed with GAD (Generalised Anxiety Disorder), a common anxiety disorder affecting about 4.4% of the UK adult population[21]. This was diagnosed in 2003 after the anxiety peaked on the back of additional pressure placed on myself during my undergraduate degree, and where I had noticed the introduction of depression and suicidal thoughts. The suicidal thoughts now included a plan of where and how. I was fortunate enough not to have decided when, but the risk was there, and I needed help. Nothing had improved, still the anxiety, and still the gastric nightmare.

In 2007, the lack of control became simply too much to cope with and so I took what I felt was a logical decision: If I reduce my food intake to near nothing, just enough food to stay alive, then I would not lose control of my bowel. If I could not control the out-take of my waste, I could most certainly control the in-take, a human being's ultimate last control. Furthermore, I knew that if I ended up in hospital, they would then see the extent of my suffering and surely must find something to help me. Any extreme in my logic can be measured against the extreme of my pain. I started surviving off one bag of rice a day and continued to exercise regularly. Naturally, the weight dropped fast. It must have been noticeable to others, since three people in my life had commented that I had lost enough weight now, and a work colleague had asked if my menstrual cycle had stopped. Eventually I had a thought… Maybe I should go to see my GP just *one* last time and really try to convey how bad life is living like this, since I would need to do it when I ended up in hospital. So, I took the leap of faith, and on my birthday in November 2007, went to see my GP who prescribed Dyhydrocodeine, a strong prescription-based painkiller. One of the side effects of this medication is peristalsis, meaning that it causes dehydration and slows the bowel down; in layman's terms: constipation. My perfect antidote! Additional side effects are that the drug is addictive, something I learned later by chance, and one of the very reasons that I have always taken it with precaution, usually as and when required nowadays, which is generally when in group situations and I need to stand up in front of people and speak. As I write this now, I have three days ahead of me when I know I will need my meds.

After taking just one tablet I felt a greater sense of control over my bodily functions, it was working. I no longer lived in fear of needing a bathroom, wondering where the nearest one is, or whether I could be in a social group and control my body. I am in no way exaggerating when I say the medication was life changing! The need for that medication still exists today, and it remains, to this day, lifesaving. The medication allows me to eat without worry that I will defecate myself, it means I can eat some of the foods that would previously have been off limits, and most importantly it provides cessation to the vicious circle of anxiety and gastric symptoms that had plagued me for years. With less anxiety, the symptoms lessened, and with less symptoms, so too the anxiety. Neither have gone away, but these are now managed, in part, by this medication. A big fear during the 2020 Covid lockdowns was whether I would be able to get my medication, and how I would cope if I ran out. Most of my gastric problems are centred around an inability to control my bowel, but from time-to-time pain can be an issue too. The pain related to my gastric problems is either non-existent or totally disabling. In the last two months, there have been at least two occasions where I have been at my company's offices and the stomach pain has started. It is like pregnancy contractions. I start to sweat, hyperventilate to breathe through the pain, and have on both occasions found myself lying on the bathroom floor of the disabled access toilet sweating and in agony.

One of those times was thirty minutes before I was due to deliver an online training course. On both occasions, my daughter (also my company's Office Manager) and one of my Associate Trainers Gemma, who also shares an office on our site, raced off and came to my rescue with anti-spasmodic medications. I can no longer take ibuprofen-based painkillers, as these have started to trigger such symptoms, and a long run (15k plus) will most certainly trigger a bout of 'runners' stomach' with similar symptoms. Lesser symptoms include occasionally feeling dizzy, light-headed and disorientated. These symptoms are common in gastric and stomach conditions.

On the back of being able to better manage my comorbid gastric problems, which Laura and I now refer to as 'The IBS Years', as she grew up alongside this, and which I am now aware is a common comorbidity (along with seizures, depression and others) for Autistic people, I was able to find my voice. I started to speak more confidently in groups and believe my voice had value too. I learned how to present to groups of people, and with the support of a great line manager at the time, I was able to co-deliver my first training course. Little did I know that this was a taste of what was to come, but not for a few years yet.

As one door closes, another opens, and one of those doors was the local NHS looking for someone who had previous experience of working with GPs (I had gained such experience during a six-month job role in a hospital after having my first baby) to manage a mental health project that worked with healthcare professionals and local workplaces to highlight and foster the health-work relationship. I applied; I was successful. The project, while fundamentally a great one, had many challenges – people, procedure, systems, culture, targets. You name it, there was a brick wall for it! My co-manager left within the first eighteen months, and I had my first and only period of workplace mental health related absence in late 2009, early 2010 – notably on the back of my painful second marriage breakdown amongst other things. The stress of work and home had bled into one another, just as it so often does for many people, and resulted in a collision of depression and anxiety.

What felt like my rescuer then emerged, my new co-manager and soon to be business partner. We clicked immediately and resurrected the failing project from the ashes, smashed our targets, and turned it into an award-winning success. We were both aware of the looming end date to the contract but had the confidence to take everything we had learned and morph that into a separate business. We did it! We set up a social enterprise and secured half a million in lottery funding to help local people with mental health problems to gain and retain employment. It was a valuable and rewarding piece of work, and our shared common purpose helped to create a strong relationship. This three-year period of my life shaped me, taught me what I wanted and what I did not want from my professional life. It also taught me who I wanted to be as a person. However, in 2015 I took the difficult decision to move on from the business.

I moved on with the intention of slowing down, appreciating life, and helping my husband-to-be with the financial administration of his own businesses. Steven had set up an IT support company in 2010, which had grown fast. This role turned out to be short-lived. Within just one month I was missing my vocation. My choice to leave the previous business was not a regret, but my need to reduce mental health suffering remained. You cannot switch off a part of you that is more than the job. My need and purpose of reducing suffering was one part of me I did recognise, though at the time I did not know why. Notwithstanding my need, I had no intention whatsoever of setting up my own company. Not until one day I happened to come across a great little training room, which turned out to be exceptionally cost-effective at £30 per day, and a little voice said to me, "If you book this room and set up a website you can promote mental health training and see if people want it. What have you got to lose?" So, the following Saturday afternoon, my IT guru husband-to-be and I came up with a business name, designed my business website, purchased domain names, and so Mind Matters was born. Six years later, my company delivers a wide range of courses, some of which I have since upskilled in to deliver, and we have around forty-five exceptionally well qualified and experienced Associate Trainers and Instructors. Our courses include Mental Health First Aid; I deliver all MHFA England's products, other than Armed Forces MHFA because I have no experience of Armed Forces life. MHFA courses train participants to become 'Mental Health First Aiders', 'MHFA Champions', and to be 'Mental Health Aware'. I deliver the i-ACT (for Positive Mental Health) programme where participants become 'Registered i-ACT Managers' and 'Registered i-ACT Practitioners', Applied Suicide Intervention Skills Training (ASIST) where participants become 'Life Assisting Care Givers' performing suicide interventions, and SafeTALK where participants become 'Suicide Alert Helpers' who identify those with thoughts of suicide. I am a Master Trainer in Dr Derek Mowbray's Strengthening Personal Resilience Training, and more recently I became an Autism Champion through the fantastic organisation Living Autism. I am proud of all these accomplishments.

Autism Awareness training will now form a new branch of the Mind Matters portfolio, as I now strongly believe it is essential that the relationship between the two fields of study is recognised and reflected in my own business. Doing so also fulfils my now ambition of raising awareness of Autism in workplaces and society. All of our courses are evidence based, they come from a strong research base, and I find training to be a rewarding and high return on investment intervention, both financially for the businesses and communities we work with, and morally and ethically. Delivering training fulfils my personal desire to reduce suffering. The website we set up that afternoon in late June 2015 is the very same website we use today, now with greater content, and a whole raft of blogs and lived experience stories. From there on in my marketing strategy was simple: throw *a lot* of mud at the wall and hope that some of it sticks!

If you were wondering how my company evolved from a time capital, cashless business to where it is today, Steven's IT Support company, 101 Digital Solutions, kick-started it with a loan of £300 for the very first order of MHFA training manuals, and my endeavours began. I set up social media pages on all well-known platforms, created my first monthly digital newsletter, and started blogging. I was active. I had systems for reaching and adding people, for seeking their following and inclusion. I made use of all the free marketing software that is out there and combined it with time. Time was by far my biggest investment, not financial capital, though many would wager they are one and the same. For a cashless start-up they are not. Our first course had the minimum eight attendees set by the licensor of the course we were delivering, which was MHFA England, and I worked hard to deliver the course to the highest possible standard. I knew those eight people would start a 'word of mouth' snowball effect that would make or break my new business. In the months that followed, I simply continued with the same process. Six years later, we deliver many more in-house 'closed' courses than 'open' public courses, but we still endeavour to run 'open' public courses for individuals. We operate an inclusive business, our 'open' public courses allow micro and small businesses to access the training where they would otherwise not be able to due to minimum delegate numbers for in-house courses. This, and the marketing power of individuals to share with others just how positive their training experience was, is the reason we run both, and the reason for our success.

The £300 was returned a year later and, like many a new business owner, I did not take an income from the business for the first couple of years, yet I was already being rewarded doing the work I love and seeing the results. I knew one thing if nothing else – just be damn good at what you do! I worked, and still work, ridiculously hard to keep my knowledge up to date, to be organised, and to do all the things that makes Mind Matters good at what it does. I live by the same ethos today. The money is simply a by-product of 'doing things well' combined with the 'difference-making' that 'doing things well' generates. And for what it is worth, I still muck-sling with the best of them so that Mind Matters is in people's psyche when they think about commissioning mental health training.

That, of course, makes something challenging sound remarkably simple. I have sweated blood and tears for my business to be successful. I have believed it possible when others have doubted me. I have proved them wrong by doing it. It is without doubt the product of Autistic obsession rarely seen at the same level in neurotypical business owners. Most neurotypicals do not obsessively-think and obsessively-behave over their business in quite the way an Autistic person might, particularly an Autistic person whose business and subject matter are their obsession. That is the ultimate reason for the successful mental health training company I have today, which delivers upwards of 130 courses each year. We continue to be a micro-business, which I am more than comfortable with, just myself and my daughter Laura as its sole employees, but with a pool of 45+ amazingly talented Associate Instructors, and one of them to whom I owe an eternal debt – she knows who she is, and she is one hell of a gem in more ways than one!

On paper I really should not be a mental health trainer. I am Autistic. I harbour a triad of impairments that includes social, social and social, difficulties communicating, and the likes. And yes, it does create challenges that would be less of an issue for a neurotypical trainer, but nevertheless, they are challenges *not* impossibilities. Prior to the 22nd of June, I did not know I was Autistic. It is quite possible that I was never meant to find out until I was forty-five; maybe the universe had a plan for me to be successful, and maybe I would not have been successful had I known earlier. Would I have pushed myself and been so determined? Or would I instead have internalised the limitations and deficits so often written and spoken about Autistics and people with disabilities? Since my diagnosis, there is a phrase that I have been unable to shake from my mind. I don't know if my brain has made this up, or if I've heard it somewhere before:

"Why can the bumblebee fly? ... Because no one told it that it could not."

I overcome my impairments because my goal of reducing suffering is worth it. The benefit is greater than the cost. I struggle with small talk at the start of my training sessions, eye contact as well, but I get by. I deliver inclusively because I know what it is like to feel excluded, and I *never*

ever force a course delegate to do anything in a group they are not comfortable with. If they just want to listen, that is their right. I deliver high quality prescriptive products that offer a structure to which I can cling. I do not like it when the licensor changes those products, or the way they are delivered, but I accept the learning curve will just take longer for me to adjust, and as of last week, I now ask for help. All Mind Matters training products have regular updates to ensure they retain quality. I actively script when I deliver training and I have honed that script over the course of the last six years. Scripting is a common trait in Autistics and is about making use of memorised strings of words, filed away in the brain, ready to be used at the right time and place. Because the triad of impairment includes 'lack of social imagination', it means we are less spontaneous, we need to plan and predict, including our words. It also means that I will probably never author a fictional book. Add anxiety to the lack of social imagination, and the challenges are compounded. So, if I have rehearsed lines that are available and ready, it makes things easier. And for my clients it guarantees a level of consistency, which is unlikely to be mirrored by my neurotypical counterparts. My training script has the best of everything within it because I can memorise high quality information. It includes facts and statistics, real life stories, and I am a self-titled 'Story-teller Trainer'. I use hearts to move minds. I appreciate many trainers will use an element of scripting and storytelling, but for me it is at a much more structured level. It is my security blanket. Take my instructor manual away and I could still take you through most of the courses I deliver and in a high-quality way because it is implicitly memorised. That said, my use of scripting can catch me out if I forget where I am. I occasionally almost use the wrong script in the wrong course, so I have to concentrate on this. Scripting does not mean I cannot answer questions and queries or go off script. Mental health is my Autistic special interest, my obsession (so too is my business), so as a result I know a lot more than most about the subject matter in hand, so questions rarely faze me. I am also not so arrogant that I won't admit if I do not know the answer to a question, but I *am* wise enough to find the answer on behalf of delegates (and myself) afterwards. I am a voracious reader and self-confessed philomath, especially when it comes to anything mental health. My motto is: 'If you are the smartest person in a room, you need to join another room!' I love learning from others, fellow trainers, course participants and others. My job is an absolute privilege.

My use of scripting is a big part of how I socially survive. Most conversations have been rehearsed in my head beforehand. I have predicted the response, yours, and my own, and so on and so forth. Some of my best conversations are the ones in my head. It is like you should have been there! I am unsure, but it is possible this is a product of both Autistic scripting, echolalia, and/or possibly Autistic stimming (STIMS: self-stimulating behaviour in the form of repetitive movements or noises). Either way, it is needed!

I told my story publicly for the third time yesterday, to a

client my company works with. Even though the narrative is mine, I own it, I do not yet have a script for telling it, though I have to say, drafting this book is helping. Because I am as yet scriptless, my Autistic brain woke me at 1am the night before and I spent two hours scripting, the scripted storytelling was repeated on my early morning run, once more in the shower, again in the car, for what must have been the tenth time, and once more before delivering the session online to over fifty people. I would not say I nailed it, but it was an improvement on the second time I told it, and most definitely an improvement on the first time, where I did not complete the story in the allocated time. Scripting is what made the third time most successful. The first time frustrated the hell out of me for weeks after. Autistic people are finishers, and if unable to do so, we will feel very incomplete and unfinished. The script is nearly there, but not fully honed yet, it needs more repetition and on a more frequent basis. I do need to get there pretty fast, though, because in two weeks I will be sharing it with the Senior Leadership Team at one of the local police forces, including the Chief Constable. Don't even get me started on my fear of authority figures!

Thanks to the mind of Henry Ford, I've spent a great deal of my life telling myself, "If you believe you can, or if you believe you can't, you are probably right." And I do find that when I can find the belief, I achieve. They are the days I want to bottle, my tens! But if there is even a sneaky level of doubt creeping in, I am screwed. It is the 'why can the bumblebee fly...' scenario. Never ever tell yourself you cannot, the mind is too powerful, it hears it, it internalises and it delivers. I find if I can visualise myself doing something I want to achieve, or if I have worked out the formula for success, then I can. I now know the formula for marathons, I know exactly what it takes, and this knowledge means I can repeat it. It is how I repeatedly pedalled out first class assignments at university; I only needed to learn the formula once. The first time is the hardest because I cannot visualise the formula, I cannot feel the formula, see the pattern. Producing a book is like that for me currently, the formula is not yet predictable. I cannot yet match the quality of my story and writing with a measured response. I can only be hopeful. How I'm dealing with the 'not knowing' is I'm telling myself to simply write from the heart. Until I have a pattern and formula I can work with, I am blind.

The combination of Autistic traits, knowledge, skills, qualification history and a driving belief in my purpose is what has made Mind Matters successful. I still make use of the admin skills acquired in school and in my early career, which are as anal and obsessive as you might expect. I had learned to touch type in school at the age of thirteen, on one of those clunky old typewriters, using carbon copy and typewriter rubbers – oh the hassle of a mistake! And God forbid your finger slipped down the side of those keys and you had to scrape it back out! For someone who does not cope well with change, I am grateful for technological advances and the benefit of backspace and delete, but thanks to those early experiences I have a typing speed of

70 wpm with about 95% accuracy. I type faster than I can write, though I think many people do nowadays because we don't really write anymore.

Like many Autistic people, I experience difficulties with executive functioning, which means I forget things – not ideal when running your own company – so I utilise lots of external prompts and reminders, lists and diary entries. I work differently to most people in that I start with the quickest jobs on my 'to do' list, rather than the most arduous like most people. A completer-finisher, I instead get all the little jobs complete, then I can fully focus on the one that needs most effort, without the visual distraction and clutter of the others in my brain. Most self-help books addressing organisational skills and time management will encourage the other way around. That is not effective for my Autistic brain. My way works for me. I also anchor things. I place objects next to the things I must remember to pick up when I leave the house, so I don't forget them. My cheese sandwich lunch – same every day – is always placed next to my bag and car keys, in my direct eyeline, otherwise I would simply forget it. If I anchor an object too soon, days earlier, it becomes white noise and I forget it anyway. I've done this with parcels and birthday cards that I need to post on a certain date. Put them with my bag too soon, get used to seeing them there, forget them as a result. I systemise and plan everything because I lack the spontaneous adaptive skills of a neurotypical – a contradiction when I've spent a lifetime adapting to fit in! In 1997 my then boss in logistics promoted me to Systems

Manager (office systems not IT) in our Traffic Office due to my ability to effectively systemise all office procedures. If I can do a task immediately, I do it immediately, or I schedule it immediately. By making use of scheduling I just need to remember one thing, to look at my diary or my 'to do' list! If a task is not documented, it is forgotten! To others it looks like elevated levels of efficiency and organisational skills, but I know the truth. One mistake I am renowned for, however, is accidentally doing a task twice, usually the ones I do immediately rather than writing the task down. I forget I have already done it, so I do it again because I worry it's not been done, and because I have no internal or external record it's been done. I have been known to write things on lists to cross them off as a record I've done them! Once a job is done, it simply goes from my brain immediately. It is usually someone else who alerts me that I have ordered the same batch of manuals twice. Better twice than not at all, I say.

I am a fast worker, machine-like in my productivity, yet my processing speed is slower. It helps if information can be shared with me in a visual way – diagrams, charts, structures, graphs, etc. If I don't have this, I am trying to build it in my mind. This means I ask lots of questions to build that image, so at times it will annoy others, especially in group situations. I need to see the big picture, a bit like doing a jigsaw. My questions are attempting to capture detail, find the missing pieces of the picture, as I am trying to visualise what is on the cover of the box without ever seeing it in full. I need information to be given in a way I can process it if I am to do what is expected. I need time to think, so put on the spot I lack spontaneity, unless it relates to an area of obsession where my picture is already vast and clear. I detest being put on the spot in social conversations and meetings if it is something I don't fully understand or I am not given time to process, prepare and script. Allistics do not generally recognise or understand these needs, and most group situations do not accommodate them.

I have a strong need to remain in control of my work, and if I cannot do so I start to experience my recurring nightmare of multiplying rodents, caged rodents that are rapidly breeding, my dream task being to keep them from escaping and procreating. If they do get out, the rodents bite the palms of my hands and fingers. I hate rats and mice. I've had this dream for as long as I can remember; it occurs when I am struggling to keep in control of my life. With a completer-finisher mentality, I get a lot done in a working day, often being more productive than my neurotypical counterparts. It is not the tasks that tire me or burn me out, it is people interactions, and I hear the same from others in the Autistic community. Time spent with people, even positive time, exhausts us. We are the slowly emptying hourglass. If there is conflict and tension it drains faster, but in either case, I still experience people-hangover, total energy exhaustion. And despite how I present to others, I am not in fact a machine. No one is.

The greatest risk that exists within my business is my own Autistic burnout, characterised by overwhelm, low mood, a fizzing pressure between my eyes, suicidal ideation, fatigue and exhaustion. The greatest challenge is I can rarely see it coming until it is there, which is something I am currently working to change, partly through rule setting. What I now understand of my depressive episodes is that they were more likely Autistic burnout rather than depression, which is why they are shorter than the average episode of depression, which is typically six to eight months. Despite the challenges, I love my work in mental health and I consider Mind Matters my fourth child. It has required similar levels of love and devotion as my children. So, to any Autistic people who are out there today doubting themselves, buying into the idea that impairment means impossible, it does not. It just means you are going to be working a little harder than most, planning more than most, eliminating as many unknowns as possible, but never forget you have the added benefit of the Au-some gene! Dream BIG, make the impossible possible, and prove them wrong! Autistic people should never be underestimated, it would be foolish to do so. They are artists, musicians, scientists, engineers and the inventors of the future, genius in some cases. A tutor (and Autistic community ally) leading a professional development course I undertook in August 2021 said he thought Autistic people were an evolutionary link, ahead of our time – I've held on to that thought as really positive.

My professional work has by its nature helped me to understand many types of mental health conditions, though my 'lived experience' extends only to anxiety, episodes of depression, self-harm in the form of overworking and masking, and likely, undiagnosed eating disorder. Despite my specialist area always being anxiety disorders, which will come as no great surprise, I have never been able to eradicate it, only manage it at best. But having a sound knowledge of anxiety disorders was the very reason I knew my diagnosis of GAD (Generalised Anxiety Disorder) didn't feel accurate. And so, I continued to search other mental health conditions. In 2019, I experienced another significant dip in my mental health, characterised by increased low mood and suicidal thoughts. At this time, I became convinced that the GAD diagnosis was wrong and that I had in fact got OCPD (Obsessive Compulsive Personality Disorder). I first came across this clinical diagnosis while studying A level psychology in 2001, while searching through a book about 'Abnormal Psychology'. At the time it resonated, so much so that I felt uncomfortable and closed the book, a book that has remained closed in my attic since. I should add that OCPD (Obsessive Compulsive Personality Disorder) is *not* OCD (Obsessive Compulsive Disorder), it is different. OCD is an anxiety disorder like GAD, whereas OCPD falls into the group of mental health diagnoses known as Personality Disorders, and the symptoms and insight are different. Anxiety disorders are episodic, they go away, whereas personality disorders are not episodic, they remain with the person. Episodic relates to 'episode of', and episodes usually comprise a development phase (becoming unwell), an acute phase (being unwell, at the worst point in the illness, and unable to do usual activities) and a recovery phase (getting better and resuming usual activity). The length of any episode can vary. It is usually dictated by how quickly someone gets help, what interventions are offered and how effective those interventions are for the person concerned. An episode therefore could last weeks, months, or even years, but nevertheless, conditions like anxiety and depression are episodic. They are neuroses and neuroses are episodic.

My anxiety had never been episodic, it was relentless, so how could it be GAD? It would need to have been a forty-five-year episode, and it wasn't without intervention! My symptoms did not fit the pattern of neurosis. I had tried lots of interventions, self-help strategies and clinical help. I exercise, eat well, rarely drink and do not smoke. My anxiety did not *ever* go away. But I did feel OCPD was much more fitting, especially as personality disorders are not episodic. It is important to add that my belief I had OCPD is an example of just how much I wanted my truth. Most people *do not* search for a personality disorder. Sadly, they are one of *the* most stigmatised types of mental health diagnosis, more so than depression, schizophrenia and bipolar disorder. The labels ascribed to personality disorders are some of the most negative and unkind descriptors in mental health. But I did not care, finding my truth and finding me was much more important than any stigma.

I am hypocritical. My self-diagnosing is a complete contradiction to the message I espouse within *all* my training courses. One of the many key messages across all the mental health courses I deliver is the participant's role is *never* to diagnose others, or themselves. Firstly, we

131

are not clinically qualified to say someone has, or does not have, a mental health condition. It is only clinically qualified professional judgement that can do that. I stand by that message regardless of my life experience, but you will note in every case where I have believed something, I subsequently sought out a qualified authority to confirm or deny the diagnosis. That said, I do not subscribe to the idea that letters after someone's name *guarantee* a greater knowledge in a subject area. You do not need to be a clinically qualified professional to gain an elevated or even specialist knowledge of a subject area. You simply need to be very well read, absorb and retain what you read, and to do so with a critical mind. Autistic people are often exceptionally adept at this, especially on any subject that has become their obsession. Many Autistics will also be obsessive thinkers, as in my own case, which is why reading and writing ease my anxiety and my mind. Reading slows my mind down, stops it obsessively thinking for a while, and allows me to relax. Reading helps me to go to sleep. Both reading and writing give me respite from my own obsessive mind.

On the back of my OCPD self-diagnosis, in 2019 I went to see a private psychiatrist in South Yorkshire. That psychiatrist led a clinical discussion that concluded with the assertion that I did *not* have OCPD, but *did* have GAD, as previously diagnosed in 2003. He added further that I had an additional anxiety disorder, which had, to date, been missed. He told me I had Social Anxiety, otherwise referred to as Social Phobia, his belief being that it had been missed because I had learned coping mechanisms to compensate for it. As it turns out, he was wrong on all counts, which goes to show, how much money you throw at a professional diagnosis in no way correlates with the likelihood of finding your truth.

At the time, I could only trust and take away with me what I had been informed through the psychiatrist's clinical judgement. I had Generalised Anxiety Disorder and Social Anxiety. And so forth I returned to the idea that I had 'managed' anxiety disorder(s), which is what I'd believed up until my barking up the wrong tree of OCPD.

Incidentally, my curiosity around the belief that I had OCPD led me to reading more about this diagnosis after my Autism diagnosis, and there appears to be a significant overlap (and misdiagnosis) here too. It is quite understandable to me now why I would come to believe I had OCPD during my search for my truth. As I see it, the only difference between the symptoms of OCPD and Autism, are OCPD describes everything I am through a negative narrative, whereas my Autism diagnosis does not. An example would be OCPD would say I am a workaholic. Autism would say my work is my Autistic special interest, which I am devoted to, and which makes me happy. I now recognise I had been very fortunate in the fact that the psychiatrist did not diagnose me with OCPD. I also believe that due consideration should be given to removing OCPD as a diagnosis altogether, especially if there is no case for any difference between it and Autism. I'm keen to understand what, if any, there is?

CHAPTER SEVEN

My Babies

Our home had gradually transformed into the rich sound of baby giggles and dreams come true. Evie and Oliver played together, though being a young mum was still exceptionally challenging for Laura.

My daughter decided to become pregnant at fifteen (yes, her teenage pregnancy was revealed as planned!) and a mum at sixteen because she so desperately wanted to fit in. She saw an identity in 'motherhood' that she believed would help her to do so. What she did not realise at the time was that there was no identity that would ever help her to feel she fitted in. The reason for this was because she too was Autistic. Had just one of those professionals taking part in the 'Team Around the Child' been Autism aware, she too would have been found sooner, but we may never have had the blessing of Evie in our lives. Like in my own case, the lack of vital awareness contributed to Laura's late diagnosis and extended suffering. Laura was diagnosed Autistic with possible ADHD on the 8th of September 2021, less than three months after my own diagnosis and with the same assessor. She is no longer lost.

Laura and I have quite literally grown up together,

because I too was young when I chose to have my first baby. At the time I thought I was old enough and mature enough, but I was neither. To be prepared to become a mum at nineteen is to be prepared to become a grandparent at a young age, as I later found.

Finding her truth has been as validating for Laura as my own was for me. Neither of us could have predicted the year that 2021 has been. Both Laura and I recognise our story to be one of extremes and both of us have felt a need to publicly disclose, in writing, as part of stripping back the mask. Publicly 'coming out' has allowed for our story to be our own words rather than Chinese whispers amongst family and friends. It delivered consistency and truth and saved us lots of repeated conversations. It also allowed us to say we are not ashamed. With Laura's blessing, I posted the following on social media:

I became a grandma at thirty-six! My eldest grandchild is now nine years old and older than my youngest children, who are eight and five. I became a mum at nineteen and had my last child at forty. At one stage my daughter and I were pregnant at the same time.

Most people don't know that about me, and the reason is because I only choose to share it when I'm comfortable with you and I feel you won't judge me for it, or my child.

I'm sharing it today because I so desperately want society to start to understand, so much so I'm actually past caring about the judgement.

My daughter decided (yes planned!) to become pregnant at fifteen and became a mum at sixteen because she so desperately wanted to fit in. She saw an identity in 'motherhood' that she believed would help her to do so. What she didn't realise at the time was that there was no identity that would ever help her to feel she fitted in. The reason for that was because she is Autistic.

Autistic people never ever feel like they really fit in, despite grasping at neurotypical ideals that we feel will help us to do so, and the reason for that is because we live in a neurotypical world that does not allow us to; your world. It does not accommodate Autistic people; it alienates us further. We adapt, we mask, but that is exhausting and causes us mental health problems, and then we get further lost in a mental health system that has not, and does not, sufficiently train its professionals to be Autism Aware. We get missed...

My daughter, like me, found her truth a year ago, and today she was officially diagnosed Autistic at the age of twenty-six! It explains so much, including why parenting her was challenging. She adds to the thousands upon thousands of #LostGirls including myself who were missed by education, health and social care. And just imagine how many 'professionals' moved in on us when she became pregnant! They ALL missed it.

A year prior to that I had reached out to the very same professionals because of the challenging behaviour I was managing at home (not knowing at the time we were both Autistic) and was made to feel like my parenting had failed. A year later when she was pregnant those very same professionals realised it wasn't simply a case of failed parenting, there were challenges within the child also, though the autistic traits were still not recognised.

So many girls and women are still lost and need help to be found. YOU could even be one of them. And I can tell you that once you get diagnosed and learn about autism you can spot it in others you meet and have known in the past. I now have what I can only describe as an Autism-dar! Those within whom I've seen the signs do not have a diagnosis; the numbers are, I believe, grossly underestimated, and most of them are female.

I ask this of you today: open your minds, hold back your judgement, think beyond what you see in front of you. Because that pregnant young lady you see may have more going on than you could even begin to know.

This (a photograph) is my beautiful daughter Laura, and eldest grandchild, Evie, who is also now awaiting her diagnostic truth, along with my eight-year-old son. Very sadly our family is once again battling for support in a system still poor in understanding Autism.

The decision to post was not an easy one, it required me to be vulnerable, and for Laura too. But its contribution to my life's purpose of reaching those who are lost was worth it. I could not have predicted the response to that post. On the professional social media platform LinkedIn, it had reached Australia within twenty-four hours. Up to press it has received over a thousand reactions, 135 comments, and has been viewed just short of 57,000 times. My inbox soon filled with requests to work for my business, people sharing that they now believe they too were autistic, or that they are already diagnosed Autistic and are still considering the merits of disclosure, particularly in the workplace. This highlighted that there are people out there who are questioning, needing guidance and support, and that the topic of Autism is very current and very real for many. For a non-celebrity, I have a reasonable audience number on most well-known social media platforms, but this is not a typical response to any of my posts on any platform. Shall we just say that if I were to judge my worth against social media 'likes' I would be extremely disappointed indeed. The reaction to this post captured my attention just as much as it captured the attention of others in my network, and beyond.

When Steven and I married in 2015, I was seventeen weeks pregnant with our third and last child. My first baby was born when I was nineteen years old and my last at forty, 'geriatric mum' printed boldly across my hospital notes the third time – yes, they *actually* do that(!) – just in case there was any confusion and people might actually think I was a 'normal' age mum, whatever that is! Our last baby went to full term – my babies like to stay put. At exactly forty weeks, I was coerced and cajoled into being induced if my baby had not put an appearance in by forty weeks and one day, or 40+1 as they like to refer to it. I had the same stretch and sweep procedure with my last birth that had kick-started proceedings with Laura twenty-one years earlier, and as previous, it did the trick. My last birth was my second easiest birth, though I was desperately exhausted at one point, about 4.30am when I was running out of energy. I constantly asked the midwife, "Have my waters burst?" Her response, "No, and even when they do it does not mean baby will be here straight away." My intuition knew otherwise. Every time I asked and every time she repeated her response. I ignored everything other than the confirmation as to whether my waters had broken. When my waters finally broke, we *both* needed no confirmation. Contraction, gush! All down her apron! She was also in the unfortunate position of kneeling in front of me listening to the bump with the foetal stethoscope. The poor midwife got a face and front full. Ben came out in less than two minutes of that happening. The nurses barely got me back on the bed in time as my baby's head was already crowning. One midwife had gone off to have her break and a sandwich. She was yelled back into the room and thrown the maternity pack as they could not open it quickly enough. If there was any competition amongst my three children as to who came out the chute fastest, my youngest wins hands down, or should I say heads down!?

All my babies were a surprise in terms of sex. No, I do not mean *that*! What I mean is we did not know whether we were getting a girl or a boy. When I was carrying Laura, the ultrasound staff did not disclose this, and with my last two pregnancies we both wanted a surprise. It was the most wonderous surprise in the world, it gives you something to keep going and helps motivate past the pain, and babies always look glorious in lemon and white. Babies have plenty of time to be genderised into a world that heavily influences this. Let's give them a chance to just be. My third and final baby was another boy, Benjamin Robert, a blue-eyed ball of chub and neck, named after my late brother Robert, who had sadly passed away the previous year at the young age of forty-one, and who never had the pleasure of meeting his doppelgänger, Ben.

As a side thought, I believe the reason Robert died young and did not get to meet his youngest nephew was in part due to his own Autism, and for many a reason I could cite, including failure within the NHS to address his symptoms early. There is a range of research illustrating Autistic adults with a learning disability are more likely to die prematurely (most commonly from epilepsy), and Autistics are more likely to die from suicide, and sometimes in childhood through infanticide – killed by parents who often cannot cope. None of this is justifiable, and the statistics are stark and unpleasant for any Autistic person to absorb. Robert was at risk of suicide several times prior to his death. He was hospitalised with suicidal thoughts and psychotic depression on three occasions in the five years prior to his death. Losing Robert has been Mum and Dad's single most devastating life challenge, for Mum the pain and loss far outweighing any impact of her own autism ten-fold, though I believe the inability to process the loss also lies in her undiagnosed autism. No mother should ever lose her child, especially a mum that is still herself lost.

Mum wasn't, of course, the only one to lose her child, Dad did too. This was made doubly worse by the fact that we also lost my beautiful paternal grandmother only six weeks earlier. My poor dad lost his mum and his son in the space of six weeks. Robert couldn't even attend our grandmother's funeral. How could he? Knowing the next time he would be in the same church would be his own. What kind of cruelty is that? It pains me to even write it. I dealt with these two losses through my faith and the belief that my nanna needed to get to the other side before her first grandchild was to pass over. I believe she is one of the many family members who is now looking after Robert. God bless her.

I try to give the boys as normal a life as possible. We go to soft play areas and parks, but I find them (the parks not the kids!) excruciatingly uncomfortable – the noise, the smells, the fast movement of little people, too many people! In fact, I detest them, but I endure them to provide normality. I feel the same about the school run and other activities where there are lots of people. Laura also shares a similar discomfort; we both find the school drop-off and pick-up incredibly difficult. I am fortunate in that my husband does many of them, but I endeavour to do a few each week because I am a big believer in fairness, and I do not think it is fair he should do all of them just because I find it difficult. The boys also ask if I am collecting them today, so it is nice for them too. I offset the imbalance by doing the lion's share of the household tasks like ironing. Unlike the school runs I did when Laura was little, where I did drop-off and pick-up daily, and where I had no friends or companionship, mums seem more friendly at Oliver and Ben's school, and I have a friend and confidante in one particular mum, who has truly understood our journey. We share a common life path, and all the trials and tribulations that go with it.

Both Oliver and Benjamin are younger than some, but not all, of our grandchildren. Laura went on to have three more beautiful children, and we are now blessed with Bella Lily, Violet Elouise and Sebastian Alexander Robert, in addition to our first-born grandchild Evie Rose, and of course Laura's husband, our son-in-law Alex. The Hudson family – Laura, her husband, and their children – no longer live with us, otherwise I would be the little old lady who lived in a shoe! Though they now have their own home, our family has a strong intergenerational bond.

Oliver and Ben have been easy to parent babies, both breastfed easily, and slept as expected. I am not saying it was in any way easy. Having babies is never easy, but our parental challenges have emerged further along the parenting journey, and overall, where Oliver is concerned rather than Ben.

At around fourteen months, Oliver started to lay on the floor, sulk and whine. A few minutes later he would be himself again, which typically was a very smiley toddler. He has the most beautiful smile and big brown eyes like his dad. Over time, these events, which I will call 'meltdowns' occurred more frequently, and became more destructive, both to Oliver and to us. They drain me of energy, make me emotional, and nowadays tend to cause me suicidal thoughts. These are passive not active thoughts, and I have safety plans in place to help me if those thoughts were to change. More on this later. I have accepted that I will have such thoughts more frequently than most because I am Autistic, and in part because I am a female who masks, which also increases the statistical likelihood of suicide. In my mind, the statistical risk factor around Autistics and suicide mirrors how many times more difficult life is for an Autistic person. If we are nine times more likely to die by suicide[22], as some research suggests, that may be because life feels nine times more difficult for us. That's a crude interpretation, which I'm sure is much more complex.

In early 2020, Covid-19 was rapidly clawing its way around the globe. We were thrown into lockdown, or as we now know it 'Lockdown One'. My business lost four months of work; all client bookings dropped to zero within the first three weeks of March 2020. With 'selective' support from the UK government – notwithstanding the campaigning of #ForgottenLtd – and the fact that I had run my business frugally for the preceding five years, we were okay. That, of course, did not stop me worrying or prevent the weekly meltdowns on my part. My husband's IT company and team were working from home, and all was quiet on the home front. All schools in England had been closed and our boys were being 'home-schooled'. I say that in the loosest sense of the word, given I was failing them daily. When Oliver is at school, his behaviour is exemplary, but at home we bear witness to several meltdowns a week, sometimes daily. Unlike my own meltdowns, which implode, where I become non-verbal and quiet, Oliver's meltdowns explode.

To the untrained eye, Oliver's meltdowns are a childhood tantrum, but they are not. It is (undiagnosed) autistic meltdown. Oliver is overwhelmed, he has reached the most he can cope with, and he is telling us in the only way he knows how. It's the type of behaviour that, if happening in public, is going to get you the side-eye from other people because *they* know their stuff. These parents are *great parents* (or if they had them, they would be!) but *you*, you have a deficit in your skill set and it is your fault, caused by you, and has failed to be rectified by you. The truth…

we are choosing our outings and battles very carefully, and in all cases actively managing the situation, though it may not appear that way to others. My brain is working through a myriad of tools and strategies, working out which will work effectively and expediently this time. I feel embarrassed; people are looking at us, at me, so my own social anxiety is going through the roof. I'm regretting my choice to take Oliver out to a public place, and I am now trying desperately to manage my own melting down and trying not to cry in public. Sadly, the failed parenting vibe prevails. It is present in other parents, particularly those who are, and have, raised neurotypical children, but rarely in those raising Autistic children. We have a shared understanding and empathy for one another's challenges. If a parent wants to see how well their parenting skills *really* stack up, they need to spend time raising a child with additional needs. Sadly, the 'failed parenting' vibe also permeates health and social care services set up to support parents, and education. They too offer a constant reminder of the deficit.

On the back of an off the Richter scale meltdown, Steven started tapping away on his laptop and said, "Jane, I think Oliver might have ADHD." No, surely not. But I am open-minded enough not to completely dismiss, so we explored the signs and symptoms and felt it worthy of formal exploration. I arranged a discussion with our GP, used the word meltdown a lot, and wondered if I was talking out of my backside throughout. I then spoke with the school SENCO (special educational needs co-ordinator) to highlight our concerns further. The GP made a referral that eventually resulted in a letter from the NHS saying… not the right department, and we recommend both parents do a 'Webster-Stratton' parenting course before we will take any further steps. In summary, we must rule out failed parenting *before* we will accept there is any credibility in the parents' concerns or need to establish a diagnosis in your child. After doing a little research online, I realised that the NHS waiting time for assessment, even after a Webster-Stratton course, could be months, maybe even years, so instead we explored the route of a private paediatric assessment. These are expensive, and we are lucky in that our savings allowed us to do this, a journey that we are still on today, and that by the end of this book I had hoped to tell you the outcome of. Yet I am unable to, but I can tell you that Oliver is not being assessed for ADHD, our original concern, but rather Autism.

Today I live with a daily fear that, despite having Oliver formally assessed in October 2021, and paying over three thousand pounds for the privilege, he will still be missed. One of my concerns is the clinical tool being used to assess Oliver is sometimes known to miss subtleties, the kind of subtleties presenting in girls. Despite being a boy, Oliver presents the female phenotype[23] of Autism more than the male. He does not 'act out' with negative behaviour in school, but rather socially masks and presents as exceptionally well behaved and subservient. Where have you heard that before?! During term time, Oliver displays obsessive skin-picking behaviour, where he peels the skin from around the tips of his fingers, because he cannot cope with the anxiety he experiences at school. During school holidays, his fingers heal. This is one of the many signs that Oliver is suffering. At the age of seven, my own fingers were the same, skin peeled until they bled.

Oliver has undergone a pre-assessment, an assessment that establishes *which* tests are recommended for him, either ADHD (attention deficit hyperactivity disorder), Autistic Spectrum Disorder, or both. The clinical outcome of Oliver's pre-assessment report can be summed up as 'possible Autism, but unlikely ADHD'. Based on this, we decided to have just the ASD assessment, rather than both. Oliver is currently midway through this process. My belief is that if Oliver's diagnostic outcome is 'not Autistic', it is wrong, and it is the process and tools that have failed to pick up on his Autism, including my own failure to convey the details of his symptoms fully, rather than Oliver not actually being Autistic. I am not, however, clinically qualified to diagnose, but I *am* his mum who knows him best. I desperately hope the process confirms his truth because I fully recognise that venturing down the NHS route when you have in independent clinical judgement that says this child is '*not* Autistic' will be even more difficult than the blank slate we started with. I will fight for his truth the same way I have fought for my own, and for Laura's.

Oliver presents with more than just meltdowns. He displays self-stimulating behaviour, otherwise referred to as STIMMING, of which there are distinct types in Autistic people. Oliver's are often stimming noises, vocal stims illustrating when he is happy. I call these his happy STIMS. They tell me he is in a good place, feeling okay. What more can any mum ask for? A set of ear defenders is what! My personal challenge is noise sends me into sensory overload. I am hypersensitive to sound, so while Oliver is okay, I am becoming not okay. These are the trials and tribulations of living in an Autistic household.

Oliver loves fast rides and anything that spins. Like Laura at the same age, Oliver still has a comfort blanket, his 'blue'. As a toddler, Oliver always used colour to describe objects, 'Mummy's white' was my car, until Mummy bought a red! He struggled with that change, but at the time we did not know why. Autistic children tend to cling to comforters much longer than Allistic children, including dummies. I refer you back to my little 't' trauma dummy extraction at the age of three, which I have an exceptionally clear and negative memory of. Oliver loves the swings in the park, another one of his stims! This is a stimming behaviour we both share. We often sneak off to the park together to go on the swings. Now I feel like I have really stripped myself totally bare! To describe how the swings make me feel is to say, "They simply make me feel alive." I could spend hours on the swings. Just like me, Oliver is also hypersensitive to light and noise, more so noise. I cannot use the hand dryers in bathrooms if Oliver is with me as he cannot cope. He equally cannot cope with the cinema due to high volume noise, or anything else that generates loud sounds. We now take ear defenders with us in case we end up somewhere too noisy for him. He cannot cope with change, even minor change. If one of the grandchildren sleeps over, he struggles with the impact of this on his routine. Oliver's sleep patterns represent those often seen in Autistic children. He is nocturnal. He struggles to go to sleep, it is often late when he eventually drifts off, and regardless of what time he goes to sleep, he is still up every morning at 6am! There are a catalogue of traits Oliver presents with, but I still fear we have not communicated this effectively to the practitioners and he may be missed. As Dr Lorna Wing highlights, a detailed history is vital. Did we give a detailed enough history, I ask myself?

As a mother I had always felt like a failure, a bad mother. It is like no matter how hard I tried, I never quite got it right. Never quite good enough. I felt like Laura had a poor childhood and this was all my fault, though Laura told me recently that this was not the case. My perception of my mothering skills has improved on the back of my diagnosis and in understanding Oliver's truth. Whilst no parent should be comparing their children, since they are all different, parenting our youngest child Ben has shown me that I am not actually a bad mum, but rather an undiagnosed (until recently) Autistic mum who has raised two thirds undiagnosed autistic children, both of whom have presented with more than challenging behaviours. Ben, our youngest, instead makes parenting feel easy, the journey is smooth and the return on investment seen quickly. He is a happy-go-lucky, confident little boy, cute in appearance, with a sense of humour that surprises us daily. He is without doubt neurotypical, he is not Autistic.

Laura and Oliver have required a much more sophisticated approach to parenting, yet I did not receive any formal parental support with Laura until she was a teen.

With Oliver, we have recently started to receive support from professionals, and that support is now increasing. Prior to any professional support, I had the informal yet valuable support of another parent whose child is diagnosed Autistic. They have listened to my woes and have shared the similar challenges they have experienced. They have signposted me to help, including online parental support groups, which have been invaluable, essential even, in the initial absence of professional support. One of those groups was an online support called Sunshine Support CIC[24], an independent award-winning special educational needs and disabilities (SEND) consultancy based in Derby. The parent, and now friend, whose own son is diagnosed Autistic, sent me a digital link one Friday night, and when I woke the following morning and began cyber-loafing on my phone, I was reminded of this. I clicked on the link and started scrolling down. At this point I too was still lost and undiagnosed, so I was stopped in my tracks immediately when I came across a post titled 'Girls with Autism'. The post, produced by Sunshine Support CIC had nineteen traits illustrated as a mind-map, a visual. Those nineteen traits were:

- Creative talents, e.g., artistic, love of writing, musical
- May appear shy
- Practises conversations in mind

- Escapes through imagination
- Trusting
- May talk a LOT about favourite topics
- May appear young for her age
- Adopts behaviour in order to fit in
- Enjoys spending time alone
- Unusual eye contact
- Anxiety
- OCD tendencies
- Routine is important to her
- Dislike of conflict
- Perfectionist
- May feel out of place in the world
- Unique sense of humour
- Unsure when it's her turn to talk
- Loves animals
- Sensitive

I read the points and cried. I had self-identified I was autistic, and my search was finally over. This time I knew without doubt that I wasn't wrong.

My search had ended through the written not spoken word. Reading is a gift that has saved my life in so many ways. I knew that very morning that I was autistic, and that morning was the start of my own journey towards diagnosis. I didn't really need more proof, but I was not qualified to self-diagnose. I owe my friend an eternal debt for assisting me to find myself, without which I may have remained lost forever. I then did what only an autistic person would do…

I wrote all the items down as headings, rated them as ten points (ten being the highest), wrote down my rationale for my meeting each trait and conducted a pseudo self-assessment of my female autistic traits. I used all points, including the first point as four individual items. There are twenty-three in total. My pseudo-assessment resulted in a score of 219/230 and this was as objective as I could achieve at this stage. I score lowest on love of animals, in the main because my fear and anxiety around animals often gets in the way of my love for them. My search had ended, but my self-identification now needed to be clinically diagnosed.

Ben, my baby, is exceptionally easy to parent, understands rules and consequence, he is easygoing, copes with change and has high self-esteem and confidence. He is the first of my three children not to cling to me at the school gates and cry. He bounces into class to be amongst his friends and is quite simply Mr Social! Ben is the only one of my three children to say, "Kids can do anything!" off the back of a "Well done Ben, that was great." I do not say that longingly, wishing the other two were like Ben, I accept they are all different. Laura and Oliver have the Au-some gene, just like me, my brother, my mum, and no doubt Ben is carrying the gene too. It may present itself in his own children if he chooses to become a parent. Ben reminds me every single day that I am a good mum, an Autistic mum raising two thirds Autistic children. I try to keep in mind that just because Ben is neurotypical does not mean that he will never struggle. I am careful that any needs he has do not go unnoticed. Ben teaches me every day how to be yourself, love yourself and defend yourself. He teaches me because at the age of five he can already do the things I have been unable to do in forty-five years.

CHAPTER EIGHT

The Many Masks of Me

"One Thing is Needful. To "give style" to one's character –
that is a grand and a rare art! He who surveys all that his
nature presents in its strength and in its weakness, and then
fashions it into an ingenious plan, until everything appears
artistic and rational, and even the weaknesses enchant the
eye – he exercises that admirable art."[25]

Friedrich Nietzsche

I self-harm, but not in the way you are probably thinking. You are probably picturing images of cutting behaviour, which is often the image most people think of when they picture self-harm. The reality is that it's a much broader range than that, which for me includes social masking, and which is frequent and equally harmful.

So why do I do it? Autistic masking is sometimes referred to as camouflaging, as it is just that. The harmful side of social masking is that it significantly contributes to Autistic burnout and increased mental ill health in those who do it. It also increases the likelihood of going unnoticed, undiagnosed and unsupported as autistic, which is also harmful. It is one of the very explanations for late diagnosed Autistic people like myself and my daughter, and for some, remaining lost forever. Worse still, social masking statistically increases the likelihood of suicide and lifetime suicidality in Autistic people[26]. It is dangerous!

Autistic social masking is a strategy developed by Autistic people for survival in a neurotypical world. The mask involves suppressing the true self, observing others, analysing and processing, learning and mimicking neurotypicals to fit in. For me, it is more than that, I am totally mesmerised by what I like to call 'Alpha-Neurotypicals', the tremendously socially successful. Alpha-Neurotypicals draw me in like a moth to a flame. They possess what I never will, social instinct! I am hypnotised by their presence and can recall every single Alpha-Neurotypical I have encountered in my lifetime. I have various social masks, some quite outgoing and even gregarious – the latter taking the most energy. I have my mental health trainer mask, and pre-diagnosis would assert, "A better person steps forward when I deliver training." What I didn't recognise at the time was that it was a presentation of one of my social masks, and possibly evidence of a diffused sense of self. I have been known to mask my handwriting to copy others' style, copy other people's clothing style, and not express what I need to say, or adapt what I say to fit an expected mask. My verbal scripts are also part of my masking, and in fact my make-up, which started out as a tool used to cover the severe acne, now forms a mask and signature of who I am. You will rarely, if ever, see me without full (but not heavy) make-up, a nude but not nude type. The only time

I do not wear make-up is when I go running. I do not mask in any way when I run, not even with make-up.

One of my biggest masking challenges is when I am in a large social gathering of friends and family, for example, our post-wedding 'get together'. Different people have seen different masks, so I simply do not know who to be in a room like that. This is when I have felt at my most uncomfortable, as it is a time when I feel most likely to be exposed and vulnerable. My daughter Laura also relates to this, she too has experienced the 'which mask do I wear now?' situation, and often must keep friends apart from one another to avoid this. The more astute of my friends and family may quietly reflect that I was a bit *out of character* at an event. Not so much a case of out of character, but which character, I ask myself. Interestingly, children can spot the lack of authenticity very quickly, and they are often the first to comment, "Mummy, you were different when…" Before being self-employed, I rarely brought my children into work or into contact with work colleagues because they would quickly expose me. I mask in front of my children as well, I suppress my natural response, which is socially anxious. I pretend to be more outgoing in the hope that my children will not pick up on my fear of people and socialising. I do not tell them that I have hidden in bathrooms at work Christmas parties to decompress, or because I am just too uncomfortable and can no longer cope. I socialise to reassure them that it is safe, even though I never feel safe in social situations, a bit like a parent who conquers a fear of spiders, or pretends not to be scared, so as not to pass the fear on. Masking is my drug, I have socially masked for so long, and do it so much, that I even mask in my dreams. Even in my unconscious state I am not my true self.

It is fair to say that everyone, including neurotypicals, mask to a greater or lesser extent. At times we are positively encouraged to in phrases like 'fake it till you make it'. As a result, many people have a fake work mask, social mask and telephone voice mask. It often goes unacknowledged, yet we all know the telephone voice mask and accent (or lack of) that we are aiming for with this, and it most certainly is not broad Yorkshire! There is most definitely accent snobbery. None of this is unusual, and many engage in the façade. Our masks are likely our subconscious, or conscious, desires of who we want to be. In my case, socially capable. When we are describing Autistic masking, however, we are referring to something that takes place for longer periods of time, and at an amplified level. I have taken the 'gold standard' neurotypical ideal and delivered it at a standard higher than most neurotypicals. It looks like success in the things I do. I have at times crafted such a successful, convincing and intriguing mask that I have occasionally sensed I am an enigma to others, a unicorn. They like what they see, and they want more; it is like they want to know the secret. These people try to get close to me, they build my trust. A common trait amongst Autistics, including myself, is that we over-trust and over share, which then makes us vulnerable. I fall for it time and again, drop the mask a little, and within a short frame of time they move

THE <i>umbrella</i> PICKER

on. It is like they wanted to see behind the mask but when they did, they were disappointed in what they saw. This is implied in statements like, "I once had you on a pedestal…" or, "I thought you were so smart, but…" the 'once', the 'but' and the 'I thought' insufficiently hidden, then their tone changes as they too realise the slip of the tongue. It's too late, I registered it. It is like they think if they rub up next to me, they will catch some of the success, or find the secret. Here's the secret: *an overwhelming desire to convince you I am neurotypical, so much so that I supersede neurotypical standards through unwavering hard work and determination.* I have now come to understand that it was never about me and a reciprocal relationship, it was more about other needs *they* had. Yet I allow it to happen because I have engineered a survival strategy that tricks both myself and others but ultimately costs me in respect of my mental health.

My life direction has also put me in situations and around certain people where I have felt the need to present a mask I do not like, a mask I have no conscious or subconscious desire to be, or to become. We must be incredibly careful of the masks we choose because we *can* become them. They start to adhere to our own flesh and being. I have borne ill-fitting masks because I have been gas-lighted, manipulated and controlled into feeling I need to, but the choice was always my own. Like too many Autistic women, I became victim to abuse, in my case subtle yet emotional abuse. Autistics are easy prey for bullies, liars and narcissists, and I am yet to meet an Autistic woman who has not been. What I am sure of is that I do not want to become an ill-fitting

158

and ugly mask, so I have at times chosen instead to remove myself from the people and situations that have made me feel like I needed to. We have the mask we present and our real mask; though different, the two need to bear some level of congruence, a common ground, particularly with our values. When I am unable to express my true thoughts and feelings, and the mask is too far removed from who I really am, it must be taken off. It is too excessive a level of incongruence. I have removed myself from certain people and situations so I can de-mask. My personal values are more important than my fitting in with some people and fitting in with a dirty mask is more than degrading.

So, what is my need? What is the driving force that ultimately shapes my masking and need to fit in? My ultimate fear is conflict, likely fed by fears of rejection and loneliness, and a belief that I am simply not loveable as my Autistic self. I am off the charts frightened of animosity.

In conflict situations, I experience panic, out of body sensations, immediate lack of bowel control, and it triggers impulsive responses and suicidal thoughts. My fear of conflict is disabling. So, as one might imagine, I will go to great lengths to avoid it, and I do. I am a diplomat, a mediator, apologetic and extremely over-thought and considered in the words I choose to avoid provocation. My last coping mechanism is silence. When I can no longer cope, I go non-verbal and low functioning. Then I meltdown. Meltdowns are not voluntary; it is heightened and extended stress that triggers them. If you have been on the receiving end of me in that exceedingly rare out of control moment, it will have built up to that point over a prolonged period, minor tensions I did not express, hurt, internalisation of unexpressed thoughts and feelings. By the time you see anything, I will have reached the stage of being unwell. This is when I act, the action is usually to remove myself from you, or to explode. On most occasions I remove myself. Over the years, I have learned that you cannot positively think your way out of toxic situations and people. I am a 'rescuer' and for a long time thought negative people can be rescued, to be shown the light. I now recognise that if their negativity is hurting me, then they must find the light for themselves. My inability to express my true self and feelings, to defend my values and beliefs, is soul destroying, so the best thing I can do is remove myself, or spend minimal amounts of time with people I cannot express my true self to. It is simply a case of self-preservation. It is the only way for me to be true to who I really am. The only people I fully down-mask around are my husband and children.

Because I mask a great deal of the time, I need lots of decompression time, time on my own to be me and to recharge. I need to be away from people, I do not want to communicate, I just want to be. I 'be' when I go running at 6.30am; an hour to be with my unmasked self.

My true self is less amenable, she is more antisocial and gets 'runner's rage' when other road users do not allow her to cross the road. She has strange routines and unusual repetitive and obsessive behaviours. She likes the texture of frozen chocolate and will only eat chocolate from the freezer, and she eats the same cheese sandwich for her lunch every day – not the actual one, of course! She cannot cope with persistent noise, bright light, or loud bangs. She collects detritus from the floor of her home, from her carpets, she cannot bear clutter or distracting out of place objects, she is 'The Umbrella Picker'. Peel back the layers of the onion and I am as Autistic as an Autistic person *should* be. Well, this Autistic person anyway. I reiterate, when you have met one person with Autism, you have met one person with Autism. How Autism affects each Autistic person will be unique to that person. 'The Umbrella Picker' is sensitive, a pattern-seeker, resourceful, and much more creative, especially when unmasked and herself. I have processed and pieced together the greatest thoughts and ideas while running because I am the unmasked version of me. I have pieced together the jigsaw of my life while running. I have authored this book in my head while running. As mentioned in my 'coming out' post, the need for such a level of 'me' time ended up in me running the 'virtual' London Marathon on the 3rd of October 2021. I ran for the National Autistic Society, and I ran 'virtual' because social masking is phenomenally exhausting, and had I been amongst a group of strangers, notwithstanding our common purpose, I would have felt the need to socially mask. Much like the fact I cannot drink alcohol and mask, I cannot run and mask at the same time either. I do not have the energy for both. And I should further add, social masking uses much more energy than the running. Autistic people who mask will tell you how constantly tired they are. My mum is always tired, my daughter Laura is always tired (but of course has four children, so Laura's tiredness cannot solely be attributed to masking), and I spend a lot of my life tired and exhausted. Morning, noon and night, I am tired. It was worse prior to 2007 when the gastric problems were at their most acute. It was a running joke amongst my second husband and his friends that I could sleep in the car from Somerset to Barnsley – like hopping in a time machine. On reflection, the reality was I had just spent a weekend away masking with in-laws, or our friends in Suffolk, and was now people hungover and totally wiped out!

One piece of the jigsaw, which slotted neatly together in my mind on a recent run, was that masking is the ultimate cause of my own suffering. If I want the suffering to end, the masking must end also. This is the inconvenient truth that a part of me has known for a very long time. My journey of demasking is going to be a long one, but one I will not shy away from because I already know it will be worth it. At least one person from the online Autistic community has already said to me in black and white terms, "Don't mask!" If only it was that easy. I simply do not know *how*, but I am working on it. Post diagnosis there has been a moderate level of unintentional demasking that is happening of its own accord. I suspect it is happening in equal measure to the gaining of self-worth and self-esteem that is also occurring quite naturally. It is also happening because I now know who I am, and I am accepting and proud of who I am. I am also proud of how I have survived not knowing who I was for forty-five years. The diagnosis has created involuntary self-development.

> *"The closing years of life are like the end of a masquerade party, when the masks are dropped."*[27]
>
> Arthur Schopenhauer
> *German philosopher (1788 – 1860)*

CHAPTER NINE

Loves, Rituals, Routines and ~~Special Interests~~ Obsessions!

At this stage in the book, it is fair to say that you will already be aware of some of my Autistic obsessions, but it would be unjust not to elaborate further and dedicate a full chapter of my book to these, since they have been a key feature of my life and survival to date.

Autistic obsessions are a well-known trait present in many Autistic people, including myself. Tony Attwood, author of numerous books on Autism, believes that not only are they present, but they have a purpose. All of my obsessions, past and present, can be linked to some purpose or other. For some Autistic people, their obsessions happen to be of a type and can develop with such gusto that they also become employment and entrepreneurial opportunities, as was the case for me with my work at Mind Matters. Nowadays many people prefer the use of the term 'special interests' or 'SPINS' when referring to Autistic obsessions. We have STIMS (self-stimulating behaviour) and we have SPINS. For me personally, the term 'special interests' is not adequate, special interests does not even come close to capturing my experience. Make no mistake, my obsessions are just that, and so forth I will use the term 'obsession'.

In and of themselves, obsessions are not harmful. Autistic obsessions are quite different from the type of obsession seen in mental health conditions like obsessive compulsive disorder. In the latter, the obsessions (described as obsessive or intrusive thoughts) are unpleasant and cause anxiety leading to compulsive behaviour (the bit that the sensationalised documentaries focus on). The obsessive thoughts and compulsive behaviour are linked and cyclic, one trying to counter the other, but the relief is short-lived and so the cycle starts again.

I am all too familiar with the types of obsessive and intrusive thoughts that are present in conditions like OCD. When I have them, my intrusive thoughts are extremely unpleasant, they include catastrophic harm to me, and catastrophic harm to my loved ones. They have been most pronounced after the birth of my babies, all three. When I had Laura, I did not tell anyone about the intrusive thoughts. I thought I was crazy, and they would lock me up or remove my baby. When I had Oliver and they emerged once more, I simply recognised them to be a feature of my relentless anxiety, so when they recurred for the third time after having Ben it was not unexpected. This time I explored them through research and a professional development training course. I learned that they were intrusive thoughts, and I also learned that there is no research whatsoever to suggest that the people who have such thoughts are likely to do the things in them. They are simply a feature of conditions such as OCD, and in my case, feature as part of my Autistic OCD tendencies and the ever-present anxiety. I also recognise them as unpleasantly purposeful. My brain shows me the worst-case scenario, so I protect myself and those I love, especially when they are vulnerable, as was the case with my newborns.

Autistic obsessions are different to these. They instead make us happy; they are positive. I feel at my most content when focusing on my obsessions. That focus is monotropic, and I can zone out most things and most people to give it my full attention. But such commitment to our obsessions sometimes means we can neglect ourselves and our responsibilities. We might forget to eat or wake in the middle of the night thinking about our obsessions. In my case, my obsessions can lead to overworking. If your obsession is your business, and your business your obsession, that business will likely be successful simply due to how much momentum sits behind it. That obsession can then create something that is difficult to contain and can become overwhelming, which is not at all healthy. Of this I need to be very aware. Whilst we need not pathologise autistic obsession, we do need to consider these factors when supporting Autistic people, especially if those Autistic people have caring responsibilities for others, such as children or pets. I work constantly to manage a healthy balance.

I've had various obsessions over my lifetime, childhood collections – dolls, erasers, toiletries; adolescent obsessions – people; and adult obsessions – scuba diving, mental health, running and Mind Matters. My current adult obsessions are Autism and anything Autism related, mental health and Mind Matters, and running, in that order. To my husband's dismay, my secondary obsessions in the form of collections are angels and anything ethereal, handbags, shoes, coats and jewellery. These collections hover in the background of my primary obsessions. They appear extravagant and materialistic, and arguably they are, but it is more than that, they offer an aesthetic beauty that is mesmerising, and they are a comfort to me. They are also hoarding behaviours resulting from 'Bag Lady Syndrome' – the fear of ending up with no home and nothing but the clothes on my back – their purpose being to exist as my plan B and perhaps hinged in my knowledge that I am my own safety net. They would allow me to raise a small amount of money and buy me the time to get back on my feet to find work, assuming the worse-case scenario ever happened! Live every day of your life frightened, and you end up with lots of paranoia and fears, and you try to eliminate and control every negative possibility. My anxiety is both pervasive and multi-dimensional.

Overall, my obsessions have so far shown themselves to be time-limited, they naturally fizzle out, and often get replaced by another one. The only obsession I have been more active in stopping was the scuba diving. I was obsessed with the idea, but it was too practical for me and I would get task overload; I understood the theory but could not apply it safely in practice. I was simply too anxious for it, and scuba diving has no space for anxiety – you make a mistake fifteen metres down that you cannot correct, you die. It was a life-preserving decision. Some Autistic obsessions can be life-time obsessions, as was the case with my brother's obsession. Robert's obsession was buses, he was a bus fanatic from a young age. Robert also turned his obsession into a career, passing his bus driving test a year before his death and successfully securing a job with a Doncaster-based bus company. He is today buried in his Wilfreda Beehive uniform and tie and took his final journey to his resting place in Thorne on a red Route Master bus, his absolute favourite! Robert did not live long enough to learn that we also shared a connection beyond that of most siblings, our both being Autistic. Losing Robert has left a gaping hole in all of our hearts. We feel robbed of a future with him, but lucky to have had him in our lives. I am proud of my brother.

My first significant obsession as an adult was crime and criminals. Not committing it myself, I might add! This too was purposeful… Imagine yourself not knowing a key part of your identity for forty-five years, maybe not ever knowing your gender, ethnicity, or sexual orientation, and at the same time recognising that you are not the same as everyone else because you always feel out of place, the odd one out. Not only do you feel out of place in the world, but you feel wrong and bad, that whatever you are is horrible. You peer into the looking glass but there is no reflection, so instead you seek your reflection in those around you for who you are. You search for answers in other planetary inhabitants like an alien in your own world. I became obsessed with crime and studying those who have committed the most heinous acts. On reflection, there is little wonder my self-worth was low. How can you love yourself if you feel so broken, wrong, excluded and bad?

Whilst I am not going to judge these people, I am not going to give them notoriety in my book. Nor am I going to look for explanations for their crimes; I did that for many years. I do not need to name the big offenders because you already know who they are thanks to a media that drip feeds us their criminality. These are the people I studied in an endeavour to find my reflection. I stared into the abyss. Thankfully, I did not find my reflection there. Nevertheless, I committed five years of my life to this search, from 2001 to 2006 – A levels, an Access course, and finally a degree in Criminology.

I studied lots of subjects during my degree: various aspects of crime and criminology, gender, ethnicity, social identity, feminism, psychology, sociology, employment law and criminal law. I became fascinated by psychological profiling, and in another life I might have made a good profiler given my human behaviour pattern-spotting. I found the whole subject matter both fascinating and purposeful. I made studying like a job. It became my obsession for around five years, and so too did the results transcripts! I dedicated myself to getting the highest possible grades, A grades at A level, with a 100% mark on a European Law exam, and first-class grades in all but one degree assignment – a Law assignment, a subject I had done so well the previous year. Getting 100% on an exam paper can leave a complacency that will catch you out, and it did, it got me a 2:1 in a first-year Law essay. I enjoyed Law, in particular Criminal Law. This would make sense since Autistic people like facts, something concrete, black and white to cling to. Overall, the outcome was a first-class honours degree in Criminology, my highest grade allotted to a criminology paper in my second year marked 92%. My lecturer handed me the result, "Well done, highest grade on record, journal quality." At post-graduate level I have achieved distinction grades, and I feel sure that my academic ability is linked to my Autism – the Au-some part, not the dark side – and is also an illustration of the monotropic focus and determination often seen in Autistics. I simply do not know how to aim lower, and do not desire to.

Many Autistic people have excellent memories, especially for anything obsession related. We can reel off facts, statistics and other information at a whim. I may struggle to tell you what I had to eat yesterday, but I can recite detailed memories from the age of two. We have probably all seen at least one online film of an Autistic person with Savant Syndrome, who as a result is able to perform extremes of memory recall. Most notable is the artist Stephen Wiltshire, who after a short one-time helicopter flight over New York City was able to draw in detail the cityscape in the succeeding twenty-four hours. A show of Autistic excellence! However, it is important to note that savant Autistics are just 1% of the Autistic population, a minority in a minority community. So, apologies in advance but I am not going to wow you with a story of my own savant excellence because I am not one of them. That said, I do share a little bit of the magic, as is often the case in the Autistic community.

During year two of my Criminology degree, we undertook what is called a 'seen' exam. This is where, a few days before an exam, the student is given one (or two in my case) essay titles to prepare a response to be written under exam conditions. I had three seen exams, so six essay titles in one week. My Autistic logic quickly determined two things: 1) I already know the formula for drafting an essay of first-class quality; and 2) actors memorise hundreds of lines for full theatre productions; the human mind is capable.

So, instead of loosely preparing for the exam, I wrote six essays of around 1300 words and memorised each verbatim. All I needed to do in the exam was write, fast! The exams were scheduled across four days. I memorised the first three of six essays – quotes, dates and all – around 3900 words. As soon as I had sat the first exam, I dropped the first two essays from my brain, memorised the fourth of six essays to go with the other in preparation for exam two, and then memorised the last two essays for the last exam, five and six. Over the course of five days, I had memorised circa 7800 words and slowly regurgitated them as fast as my hand could write. And I forgot all of them as quickly as I had memorised them. The only thing I can recall today is that one essay related to environmental criminology, street lighting and the likes. I received a first-class grade for all three seen exams. My memory recall is a visual one. I simply recalled the information based on where I had been when I learned it, or a particular section of the essay based on any creases in the paper, the shape of the sentence or paragraph, or splodges of ink and crossings-out on the page, all visual aids. This I believe is termed anchoring, attaching the information you want to recall to something else. I think in pictures and stories. If you want to explain something complex to me, show me it in a picture. Then give me time to process that information. Unfortunately, that is as good as I will get to Savant excellence. I am such a contradiction. I can memorise huge chunks of words yet need external prompts so that I do not forget things like ordering a set of training manuals for a course or remembering someone's name! An ex-colleague once highlighted: "You don't remember people's names, it's like you don't care…" then realised the offence and finished with a less accusatory, "… but that can't be right because you do." They too recognised the incongruence but could not unpick the contradiction or fundamental issue. One person suggested to me that they knew me better than I knew myself. On reflection, I now recognise why a comment like that would feel so painful to a lost girl. I wish they had. My search would have been over much sooner. My exceptionally good and exceptionally poor memory is a perfect example of the communication challenges and high and low functioning paradigms in Autism. I can be both high *and* low functioning, I am neither one nor the other, and yet I am both. Measure me against one or the other and you would be wrong in both at certain times. Our functioning is fluid.

So having not found my identity in the depraved and immoral of society, I drifted. Along with my manoeuvre into the NHS and managing a mental health project, I started to build knowledge and greater interest in mental health. I yearned for more understanding, particularly around anxiety disorders and diagnosis. I sought out the people with knowledge, the literature, the journals of value, and immersed myself into my new obsession. The one thing I would come to learn in recent years was that my diagnoses could not be correct. They were like an ill-fitting dress, something that just wasn't right. My obsession in mental health remains today, regardless of any diagnosis, though it is now less about the searching and more solely about the purpose of reducing suffering in others. This obsession can no longer operate alone, however, it is now inextricably linked to Autism. That being so, one of the things I am constantly making the case for is a greater understanding of Autism amongst mental health professionals. I remained lost for too long because of a lack of understanding, and others remain so because it continues. But one thing I have always been aware of is that if you want to have a voice about something, you have got to stack up on credibility. I am hoping my book gives me a personal authority on myself and my Autism, with some authority on the subject matter, but just to remind you there are no experts in Autism, because every Autistic person is different. Whilst there are no experts, there *are* leading authorities, and one day I would like to become one of them. There are too many unanswered questions for me not to pursue my interest further.

I am totally obsessed and immersed in Autism. It keeps me awake at night with obsessive thinking. It is the last thing on my mind when I go to sleep, and the first thing on my mind when I wake. The devotion given to my obsessions is unparalleled. I cannot stop it, and nor do I want to. I cannot tell you just how many times since diagnosis I have found myself sitting in my easy chair alone during the early hours reading in the hope of shutting down my over-active brain. All because I woke to go to the bathroom and my brain thought, "Hey, let's play Autism! Who cares that it's 2am!? Anytime is good to think about Autism!"

Thanks to my self-titled 'sleepy teabags', I am usually able to go back to sleep, but often at the cost of my early morning run. You cannot be awake thinking for hours during the night and up at 6am running 10k! Even I am not a total machine! This very paragraph started out in the notes of my iPhone at 00:11 when I needed to pee! Autism is my current obsession. Make no mistake, this book is both the product of a desire and quest to find lost girls – a passion borne of and in equal measure to my pain and suffering – but also a product of Autistic obsession! Autism for me will now likely form a 'lifetime obsession' that will remain with me for the second half of my life. I am already aware of a related desire (yearning even) to return to academia to study Autism at post-graduate level and beyond. You see, one of my coping mechanisms is to learn as much as there is to know about a subject in order to cope with it, whether that is a person I am trying to cope with, a condition, or otherwise. If I am to cope effectively with my Autism, I need to understand it from the inside out, and to understand the 'Autistic me' from the inside out. I had no prior desire to return to academia pre-diagnosis. My interest will end when I have answered some of the important questions that crosscut my own and others' experience, and which currently remain unanswered. There are so many. Enough to keep an obsessed Autistic mind occupied for the rest of its living days. Sadly, I do not have the years left in me for the dreams I have now. I have been locked away in a prison for forty-five years, and now I have been released. I have what is left, and you can be sure I am going to make the best of it!

I now want to shape the future of Autism understanding, not just through this book, but through empirical research. I will always struggle with the guilt that there are people in my life whom I love with all my heart, my husband, my children, yet it is my obsessions which consume a bigger space in my mind. I cannot switch that off, and the fact that I do not want to makes me feel more guilty. At least I now have an explanation for this need, an explanation that does not include... maybe I don't love them enough? As an Autistic person, my obsessions are my basic needs. I need them like the air I breathe, so that I can survive *and* love those who are also my world.

I am loquacious, and given the chance, will wax lyrical about my obsessions. I would like to publicly apologise to the local Chamber of Commerce networker at a recent Patron's Dinner with whom I could not do small talk, but instead manipulated the conversation into a heartfelt deep discussion about Autism, to the exclusion of small talk with the rest of our dinner table! As an Autistic person, I cannot do small talk. I run out of script, but anything 'meaning of life' and I'm your girl. The gentleman was gracious and reciprocating, but still, I chastised myself afterwards. This was one of my many social faux pas, a lesser one in fact. I do know the social rules, I can tell you what I *should* be doing, but I cannot deliver, so instead I engineer something within which I can cope. I also engineer *authentic* conversation, notwithstanding my masking! I find small talk superficial, over-produced, and false. At the very least there is an honesty to the conversations I have.

To manage my well-being during the Covid pandemic, I started running. This is something I did prior to having my last two children. I had exercised regularly for about ten years, then my other obsessions – mental health and Mind Matters – took over. Mind Matters lost four months of work and income from March to June 2020 because all of our training products were face-to-face options only, and we were no longer allowed to be in contact with people in a training room due to the virus. By July 2020, the licensed products we deliver had been adapted for online delivery, which allowed us to commence regrowth and put us back on track. The marketplace is still volatile, and as a business owner, I *never ever* rest on my laurels. But the change brought about some benefits, more free time, no more long-distance commutes and logistical challenges, no more staying in hotels four times a month, and with this I decided to better manage my anxiety through running.

To begin with I did less than a mile daily, so nothing over ambitious, but Autistic people need external motivators, so before I knew it, I had signed up to the 2021 London Marathon, and was running 11k five mornings a week. I run in rain, snow, ice and sunshine. I love running in all weather and all seasons! Signing up for the London Marathon is another illustration of me trying to prove (unsuccessfully) through extremes that I am neurotypical while not being neurotypical. During this time, I was still undiagnosed. As I write today, it is October 2021 and since February 2021, I have run over 1200 miles. I have run more miles than I have driven in my car this year. So, as mentioned in my 'coming out' post, on 3rd October 2021 I ran the 'virtual' London Marathon. The virtual marathon was well thought out, with start and finish timers just the same as those running in London. There was location commentary that could be piped through your earphones, so you could visualise being on the London route just like the other runners (should you wish to experience that; I was happy listening to an audiobook, running in my hometown of Barnsley). The virtual runners were helped to feel connected with fellow runners in our unified purpose. I thoroughly enjoyed the marathon, which I completed with just one fall at twenty miles, leaving me with one grazed knee, one sprained hand, which needed to be X-rayed two days later, and a grazed shoulder. Oh, and a missing toenail, an occupational hazard for most long-distance runners! With my ego just about intact and a husband who had my back throughout, I finished in four hours fifty-four minutes. Running the iconic London Marathon had been on my 'to do' bucket list for around twelve years, and I just wanted to achieve it once. I was satisfied with my efforts, and I came away with no desire to repeat it… not until one Monday morning later in October 2021, when driving to work my brain said, "Hey, do it once more, but this time do it live! Drop the mask, do it!" The London Marathon ballot had closed eight hours earlier, so my timing was exceptionally poor. As a result, I now have an application submitted to run for the National Autistic Society in 2022, and by the time this book goes out to market I will know whether I am running for them or not. It seems I can do nothing by half measure, and nothing just once!

As an Autistic person, I have routines, lots of routines, and they help me feel safe. Routine is illustrated in my running and the fact that I run the same route every time I go out. I cross the road in the same place, I know exactly how many roads I need to cross, the lumps and bumps in the road, and that makes me feel safe. Running live in London will take me 'off route' and away from my routine, which I will find difficult. For this reason alone, the live London Marathon will be more difficult. My husband has on several occasions attempted to encourage variety into my training, to no avail. I need routine. Broken routines also cause me a great deal of stress and discomfort, whether that is interruption to plans, phone calls, or otherwise. All can throw me off plan. Most neurotypicals deal with change and interruption reasonably well, but for me, even a small change can upset the rest of my day.

You would have thought my two big obsessions of crime and mental health would be enough, but they were searches, and I still had not found what I was looking for. As someone who is open-minded, I had in no way ruled out the possibility that the crux of my suffering could be outside of this lifetime…There is nothing that makes me happier than a bookshop, and a second-hand one at that. Back in the early noughties, I had visited one in Glastonbury, not too far from where my in-laws lived at the time, and where we had spent many a wonderful Christmas and weekend away. I had picked up a book called *Life Between Life* by Joel Whitton[28]. It was a tough read that I persevered with, a read that made the case for our souls having traversed many bodies (the vehicle), and that we continue to return to the earth plain (in new vehicles) because there are things we still need to learn. It also makes the case that between those lives, we are placed in a spiritual waiting area – this was the focus of the book – the life *between* lives. That book moved me, and its content has remained with me, in part because there were some horribly graphic stories and, for me, they caused intrusive thoughts. But that book opened my mind to the idea that it might not be about this lifetime alone.

I had always been open-minded and interested in spirituality, and on the back of my second divorce I decided to attend my local spiritualist church. I had wanted to go for years, but never plucked up the courage. One Friday night, I found my courage and I walked into my local church and received a very warm welcome. I now recognise that on that particular night a message came to me, via the medium, from a deceased relative of my ex-husband. It was the first message the medium delivered. I did not know I had to verbally agree to 'take the message' and so forth it was lost to no one in the room. But I soon realised the spiritualist church protocol and now know when to 'take' a message. I still attend now and again when I have time, and I still receive the same warm welcome whether I attend once a year, or twenty times. I have since had private readings, group readings and attended many an open-circle, or performance of mediumship. This very weekend I attended what is called a Trance night – about as left field as they come, even for me! Think Whoopi Goldberg and *Ghost* when her character is consumed by Sam Wheat. I have also had my own direct messages, often sent to me via songs and their lyrics. This year it was Years & Years with their song 'The Shine'. For months, I constantly felt compelled to listen to it, especially when I had been running. I even nicknamed it my running song. About two months after diagnosis, my slow-on-the-uptake brain *heard* the lyrics say that it was you I had been waiting to find. Ta-da! The penny had dropped. It was telling me I would find my truth and even looking at the band name now, that too speaks volumes in terms of how long I had been searching. Once the message is registered on a cerebral level, I no longer feel the urge to listen to the song. It's like spirit are satisfied it got through. This is not the first time a message has been delivered in this way; the last spirit message delivered via song was Pink's 'Who Knew' in 2006, warning me that in three years from now my second husband would be long gone. I'd had a twinge of knowing at the time, an inconvenient truth, but only fully connected with the lyrics three years later. My second husband left me early 2009. Stevie Wonder's 'Isn't She Lovely' was telling me I was pregnant on the way to Scarborough for my stained-glass craft retreat. I have also been told by a spiritualist medium that I receive messages through song lyrics.

Just before any non-believers condemn me as airy-fairy, and my beliefs nonsense, I should say I am a very logical and empirical thinker. Despite that fact, there are some experiences I simply cannot explain through science alone. And for what it is worth, I *always* attempt to find explanation through science first. When I have process eliminated to the nth degree and I cannot find the answer in science, I am left to assume it is beyond either my empirical mind, or this world. I should also say you can no more disprove the existence of the spirit world than I can prove it. You cannot prove, for example, that God does not exist, no more than I can prove God does. That is faith, faith in what we believe.

My spiritual belief draws me to anything angelic; our cat is named Angel, though she is so far removed from ethereal we should have called her Satan. For the last week she has taken a poo daily in our bedroom, suddenly deciding that behind our bedroom door is her spot! She has a litter tray! She also brings us daily gifts of mice, rats, voles and shrews! You might be reminded that my recurring nightmare is multiplying rodents.

In my quest to find answers in the spirit world, I also became fascinated with the work of Dr Brian Weiss. I had ordered a batch of books from an online book company, and in doing so was offered a free loyalty book. I simply added a random book to my basket, which I absolutely judged by its cover! That book was called *Same Soul, Many Bodies*[29] by Dr Brian Weiss. On receipt, I tossed it aside, thinking it would be trite and hardly worth my time. Eventually it became the unread book, so I changed that.

Through that book and the rest of Dr Brian Weiss' published works (I have since read them all), I was introduced to the idea that suffering in this lifetime can be anchored to events in a previous lifetime and that the imprint of that suffering can be brought forward with the soul into the new body, or new life. It remained with the soul during the life between lives, and carries on. Those of you around in the eighties may remember 'Galileo' by The Indigo Girls. Same thing, explained through song. Like myself, an empiricist, Dr Weiss could not explain his psychological practice experiences through science. During hypnotherapy, he accidentally took a patient back to their past life by asking them to go back to the source of their suffering. It turned out *not* to be in this lifetime. Having read all the books, I had started to believe my problems were in a previous life – what the hell had I done wrong!? I dragged my husband along to see Dr Brian Weiss at a Hay House event in London and considered whether to extend my searching to 'regression therapy'. For a time, I was obsessed with anything spiritual. Fear stopped me taking the regression stuff further, and an underlying belief that my answers were in fact in mental health rather than past lives.

I was raised Church of England, though not strict Church of England, but its sentiments remain with me too. Our children attend a Catholic and Church of England co-educational all-through school, but I consider myself Spiritualist and I practice its principals every day. It is a benign religion in that humanity has never gone to war over it, unlike many other religions. As a pacifist, this is attractive to me. I simply have an unfettered belief in something bigger than me. I think there is a possibility too that lost and undiagnosed autistic women may be drawn to all things Spiritualism in their quest to find themselves, whether they are consciously aware of that, or not. I see a pattern there.

So, crime, mental health, running, spiritualism, they've all been, or are, my obsessions. I also have other unusual habits, which I would not necessarily call my obsessions, but I do find them pleasurable or ritualistic and necessary. For example, reading and pronouncing the long chemical names on the back of toiletry bottles when I am in the bath. I love the way the chemical names feel in my brain and my ability to pronounce them. I am also superstitious, so I regularly salute magpies. I have driving rituals, so every time I get in my car and drive, I *always* pray: "St Christopher, protect this journey, protect me and other road users, and keep my vehicle safe from damage."

I am intensely scared of driving in the snow – I

pray and chant as I drive. If I can avoid driving in snow altogether then I do, but my work has made avoidance not always possible. I say the same prayer when I go running, my vehicle in this case being my body. This I guess is both religious, habit formed and ritualistic. And likely fuelled by anxiety. If I am due to be delivering training on a given day I also pray: "God, angels, spirit, spirit guide, nannas, grandads, Robert and other spirit who care about me [I don't want to miss anyone out] please help me to deliver a really cracking course today. Protect me from negativity, put a veil of blue light around me and my course delegates. Help me to be able to answer any questions. Put an angel and a dove on everyone's shoulder. Help me to keep to time, not to have any technical problems, be clear and eloquent, and to deliver the values and messages of the course so that the delegates can get the best out of the training to help themselves and others. Help me to make a difference to everyone in that room (or online), and to myself." Then the Lord's prayer to solidify it all. I sometimes use a similar prayer when I am going into uncomfortable social situations. This is obsessive and ritualistic, possibly more a sign of my anxiety and obsessive-compulsive tendencies than any religious conviction, but I genuinely believe that a considerable proportion of my success is down to the support I receive from beyond this world, as well as any effort I myself put in. Make of that what you will. I am always mindful that others may not share my spiritual beliefs. I am not for a moment suggesting you all become spiritual. I am merely sharing examples of my own behaviours, some of which happen to be spiritual, some of which may be pinned down to my Autism.

CHAPTER TEN (A)

What They Don't Prepare You For

If asked prior to my official diagnosis whether I was prepared, I would have wholeheartedly said, "Yes, of course!" and how wrong I would have been. When you have searched for so long, fathomed things out for yourself, and you are now waiting for the seal of approval, the last part simply seems like a formality. Your official ticket into a system of support that, without which, you are largely excluded from. Society needs a label.

Prior to my diagnosis, I was label averse. I had explored Labelling Theory[30] during my degree and the potential damage labels could cause. I did not consider myself a label seeker, quite the opposite, in fact. I believed that some parents and carers actively sought labels for their children to mitigate their own poor parenting, or to excuse their child's behaviour. What I now believe is, that which I might have thought was poor parenting, or a child having a tantrum, is not *always* the case when you dig a little deeper, and secondly, when a label is an *accurate* label, it has the potential to be positively life-changing, as was the case for me. I am no longer label averse; I am misdiagnosis averse.

What no one could have prepared me for was the

neurological shift in my brain that took place when Deborah told me I was Autistic. As a person who thinks in stories and pictures, I visualise my brain shift as giant steel cogs, some upright, some horizontal, all working together and shape shifting neatly into a new pattern of knowing, like the changing of gears. The psychological shift was seismic, and it was fast. My mood shot through the roof to levels of euphoria akin to mania. No, thank you, no misdiagnosis, I am merely conveying how elated I felt. I knew these feelings could not be sustainable. And so too they weren't.

Over the weeks that followed, I felt like I was on an emotional roller coaster of highs and lows. I would simply burst into tears, mostly happy tears, but also tears of self-compassion for my suffering, for the umbrella picking little girl who suffered for too long. I now have a compassion for my inner child not previously seen. There were tears of acknowledgement, memories clicking into place, and everything now making sense. Tears of exoneration that I am not bad or horrid. It still happens now and again, but now the tears are self-compassionate tears, sometimes laced with anger for the unnecessary suffering I have undergone, which could have ended sooner. I am as profoundly aware of my loss as much as the gain. Like 'Stockholm syndrome' – where victims form emotional attachments to their captor – I too was leaving behind a part of me, albeit a part of me that was dark, but nevertheless a part of me that I was still attached to, an identity that I had lived. Not having an identity, not having your truth, is still an identity. The identity I had was 'Lost Girl'.

I recognised quite quickly that I was moving through the cycle of grief. I was experiencing a loss, a bereavement for the person that was, but wasn't.

The Five Stages of Grief[31] model developed by David Kubler-Ross, a Swiss-American psychiatrist, and Elisabeth Kessler, suggests that when processing grief we go through the following five stages:

- Denial
- Anger
- Bargaining
- Depression
- Acceptance

How long we remain in each stage will be dictated by many variables. Some people will go through the five stages more quickly than others. I have seen my own mum in all stages of grief, with the exclusion of acceptance, the stage I pray she will one day reach. Sadly, due to losing her son, and her mum, she is currently locked in a depression with no clear pathway out. I also suspect that Mum's undiagnosed autism is playing its part in this. Karla Fisher (2012) in her online article 'Autistic Grief is not like Neurotypical Grief'[32] highlights the additional challenges Autistic people face when processing grief. (If you want to read more this is her article http://www.thinkingautismguide. com/2012/08/autistic-grief-is-not-like-neurotypical.html). Everything about life is different for Autistics, the way we experience love, loss, change, everything. In respect of my own post-diagnosis grieving process, the move into denial was almost instantaneous – characterised by the moment of, "OMG this cannot be right, can it?!" I was in that stage for just a few days. The anger stage, I waiver in and out of. I am not sure I am fully done with it yet because I still get angry that I have lost so much of my life to not knowing. As I am self-editing and reading this text back right now, I am crying again, crying because I have a chance at a future so much better than my past. I feel so incredibly lucky, they are tears of joy.

I also have moments when my mood plummets, often with the recognition that I will live every day of the rest of my life with anxiety. A cure will now never be possible, and with that comes an inevitable loss of hope that had always existed. I had always believed that if I searched hard enough, I'd find an answer, a solution to my anxiety. Hope is never a flame we want to extinguish. I move towards acceptance but hover in and out of this too, more in than out. I am quite sure I am somewhere mid-cycle, but the process has by no means reached its zenith. Many recently diagnosed Autistics also talk of the grieving process, I know I am not alone in this. Knowing I am no longer alone has also contributed positively to the healing process.

Following my official diagnosis, I decided to join the online Autistic community, and what a great support they have been! I had chosen not to up until diagnosis, mainly because a part of me was frightened I could still be wrong. I did not want to join a tribe, to engage and embrace them, and find out I had no legitimacy being there. I had lived like

189

an alien amongst my people for too long already. With this tribe, I knew I needed to fully belong. It just wasn't right for me until I was formally diagnosed. The online forums are not solely for those officially diagnosed Autistic, many in fact are frequented by people who are *self*-identified, or enquiring for a friend, but for me I needed the authenticity of the diagnosis first. The online Autism community have provided me with a safe space, support, understanding and guidance. They are one of the rare online communities where you do not see lots of conflict and overbearing egos, and they are incredibly knowledgeable! I feel at home in these groups, and I feel proud to be Autistic. Why? Because I have found my people, *my* tribe. Adult Autism groups, parents of children with Autism groups, Aspie groups, ADHD groups, and a mix of other neurodivergence groups, *all* my family, my brethren. I am loyal to them and consider myself their friend and ally if they ever need my help. I will shout for my people, be their voice if they ever need one, be there to lean on when it is too much.

I feel I have been reborn into a new world with a new perspective, but my past life memory remains. Each time I think of a memory, I slot over my new Autistic lens – optician style – and reanalyse it for variance. The new image will almost certainly have a new take on the old memory, there is *always* a change, it becomes reframed. This is happening to me all the time, it may happen for years yet. I call them my 'ah-hah!' moments when the cogs engage in a new pattern. Very often nasty images and memories are neutralised. I have forgiven myself and I have forgiven others. That does not mean I will allow a repetition of my past, I most certainly will not. But forgiveness is the ultimate strength anyone has, it frees us, and others, and we all have it within our power to forgive. Recognising your worth allows you to forgive. For some people that will mean forgiving God or asking for God's forgiveness, for others simply forgiving themselves. Because I have now forgiven me, I will not ever again let myself be a victim of other people's egos, manipulation, or control.

My 'coming out' was another fundamental need that I had following diagnosis. It did not happen immediately; it was more of a growing need that I could eventually no longer contain. I am comfortable with disclosure, mainly because it links to a greater purpose for me. I have for a long time been comfortable in talking about my mental health difficulties, so my Autism is simply an adjunct to that. That said, I can convey my lived experience in writing more effectively than I can verbally, something you might expect given my challenges with social communication and 'alternative' wiring. One of the reasons for this is I do not, as yet, have a script for it. I know my life story, my narrative, but I do not have a script for public speaking my story. It will come, it will get honed, just like my training script, and when it does it will be proficient. The dream... a TED Talk; yes, that is the verbal dream if I have one, ever more so because I know the challenges I would need to overcome to do this. If you do not know my written dream by now, you may as well close the book.

Following my diagnosis and the shift in my own

brain, I shared my truth with others. For some this may have created a sizable shift in their own psyche, but not all. Mum was surprised by my diagnosis, and sadly blamed herself for not having noticed it during my childhood. She blames herself for my past. Several people highlighted to her that the world back then did not know what it now does about Autism. It is no one's fault, and blame will not change anything. Learning and forward progression is instead what we need. Over time, Mum has recognised the diagnosis has been a significant positive change, and our relationship is now the strongest it has ever been. I love Mum, and I do not tell her this often enough. Dad too, so just in case either are reading this and missed it – I LOVE YOU BOTH... and so did Robert. This is something I struggle to express verbally but can do so more easily through the written word. It does not matter *how* I say this, it matters that I do. Understanding my own Autism has helped me to understand Mum in so many ways, her five vacuum cleaners, her need for space, her big heart, how other people's pain weighs heavy on her, and her obsessional needs. She is autistic too but does not want her seal of approval, which I would have helped make happen had she wanted it. She does, however, own her identity now, and I remind her it is okay to manage her boundaries, protect her obsessions, and say to others, "No I cannot do that." She speaks with more honesty to me, and me to her. We are both able to say we need to adapt things, and both able to accommodate the other person's needs when that is the case. We have more compassion for each other. I don't believe we were able to do this prior to knowing the truth. I would never have predicted that finding my truth would have such a positive effect on relationships, ones that could at times be very strained.

To cope with the processing of my diagnosis, I did what many an Autistic person would do, and that was to learn and devour facts about the subject matter. My thirst for Autism knowledge was, and still is, insatiable. I consume books, watch films, search out blogs and websites. At the start of reading other published works, I thought, 'wow, these people know a lot about the condition and neurodiversity'. Their minds were so impressive. I think I'm slowly becoming one of those people. I am by no means whatsoever an expert on Autism, partly because there *are* no experts, and partly because there are so many with phenomenal understanding. But even Simon Baron-Cohen or the late Dr Lorna Wing, Hans Asperger, or Leo Kanner, even they are not experts. Why? Because every single person with Autism has a different constellation of traits, it is complex. We can at best be an expert in our own Autism, but not others'. There is still a great deal of research that needs to take place, especially when it comes to women with Autism, my personal area of interest. My interest in women with Autism, combined with becoming more Autism aware, brought about another unexpected post-diagnosis development – my neuroscope!

My neuroscope picks up on the signs and traits of Autism in others. I had started to notice that I could recognise other people with it, especially other Autistic women, and girls in some cases. My neuroscope had developed because I can absorb and retain facts, and because I pattern-seek based on that information. It was almost as if I were internally diagnosing everyone around me, my daughter joking, "They should give you a job on the ASD assessment backlog, you'd bottom the list within a week!" Surely that could not be right, could it? Not everyone around me is Autistic? Otherwise, we would *all* be Autistic! The answer is no, indeed they cannot. But I had not yet worked out the pattern I was witnessing. With my analytical overthinking brain, it was coming...

During a run, as you might expect, my brain thought, "Ahhhh, no, not *everyone* is Autistic, but rather Autistic people move in and amongst their own tribe, they connect best with their own people. Their friends, if they have friends (Autistic people tend to have few if any friends), will also likely be Autistic, their life partners, husbands, wives and others who connect well with them. I could also see this in Oliver and the friends he connected with, children hiding in plain sight from adults who were not Autism aware. That very same day I undertook an online course called 'Basic Neuroscience of Autism'. I put my theory to the course leader for his thoughts. Before he even had a chance to respond to my question, the other participants crashed the chat box with messages of, "Did you not even know that?!" One person cleverly created an image of a magnet. The chat responses solidified my theory. Many of my fellow participants were diagnosed Autistic, and clearly, they were light years ahead of me!

Within two months of my diagnosis, one of my best friends was also officially diagnosed Autistic – another late diagnosed female, and since then a friend of hers too, and so the chain will continue I'm sure. Early on in our relationship, I remember a conversation where we were talking about hot bath water and the fact that when you put your foot into the water your brain cannot always compute whether it is too hot or too cold, my friend saying, "Yes, it's like your brain can only register extreme, but it cannot identify *which extreme*!" I recall at the time that small statement blowing me away, one of the very reasons the conversation has stayed with me. It told me my friend's brain was a considered one, and that she had worked out that the brain could be fallible in its processing. Fallible processing in fact turned out to be 'different' processing for both of us. My friend is one of the smartest people I know. If I am seeking a mind-blowing conversation, she is my go-to friend who will always fulfil. On reflection, that cursory discussion revealed something else: we both had sensory processing challenges not experienced by others, and we both understood one another. We connected because we were *both* Autistic! Both our diagnoses came twenty-three years after bath talks, at the ages of forty-five.

I also now recognise undiagnosed autism in other close friends, autistic traits, ways of being, the fact that we 'connect' and do so exceptionally well. The fact that I can remove some of my mask when I am around them tells me I am more comfortable in their company than the company of neurotypicals. In one case, our shared traits were (now laughably) put down to us having the same horoscope sign. But on an early morning run, my overthinking brain said, "Nooooo, you are not obsessive because you are both Scorpios – you are not living in a Facebook horoscope meme *eye roll* – you are obsessive because you are *both* Autistic!" *Second eye roll* It is like my brain was taking the piss out of me. "Come on, Jane, wake up and smell the coffee!" I guess this is an example of my slow processing. I always remember the American television series *Superman* televised on a Saturday evening during the late nineties where Lex Luther is trying to illustrate that Superman and Clark Kent are one and the same – spectacles on, spectacles off – with everyone around him looking vacant and slow on the uptake. This is me and my 'oh yeah!' or 'ah-hah!' moments, my intellectual climaxes. I am such a contradiction at times, bright and stupid all rolled into one!

So, I had started to work out who amongst my close friends was autistic as well. I currently have five close girlfriends. All of my close friends are female, and I regularly describe myself as a woman's woman. This may explain why I can spot the traits more easily in women than men. Going back fifteen years or so, I had seven close girlfriends. Of the five that remain, in my opinion, only one is neurotypical, and that friendship is my longest-standing friendship.

When I first met Sam, I was fifteen, Sam seventeen, and we were in our first job following school, working at a motor trade training centre. We both originate from Thorne, so this was our common ground for a blossoming friendship. Sam has seen the good, the bad and the ugly of me, yet never fully seen under the mask, just like my other close friends. This disheartens me and leaves me feeling dishonest and lacking in authenticity in my friendships. God bless my friends for accepting that. Sam and I have shared life's ups and downs, we've laughed, cried (mostly me), enjoyed a shameless love of handbags and shoes, and shared many a delightful meal together. In the early days, it was KFC. Today our palates are a tad more refined and our eating budget more accommodating, though Sam will almost always have a voucher, a two-for-one, or loyalty points. I believe Martin Lewis is her all-time hero! Sam's daughter, my goddaughter Grace, makes me an enormously proud godmother, as does my godson Matthew. I consider them my extended family.

I learned early on that I am immune to compliments, even from friends; they are too subjective. I do not really absorb them, but I will mask that I do. I know to thank people and graciously accept them, to do what is appropriate, but it is merely a façade not to upset others. Instead, like many Autistic people, I take my compliments from external and objective reward. I require external motivators, and for me this has resulted in a collection of accolades – qualifications, medals, letters after my name, and measurable achievements – visually and tangibly measurable. This can look 'showy' to others, and if you are regularly around a person like that, and your own self-esteem does not happen to be as robust as you would like or as robust as you believe it to be, then you can start to feel lesser or inferior. Such feelings are the foundation for jealousy, one of the emotions that can easily start to develop. When this happens, response behaviours can become competitiveness, control and sometimes abuse, anything to reduce the other person back down to how they feel. I have no control over other people's response to me, only my response to others and events. Someone else's jealousy is theirs to resolve (if they wish to) not mine. When I have been on the receiving end of such behaviour, I have usually removed myself from that person in order to survive.

On the back of my autistic identity parade, I recognised a pattern. The reason my close friendship number has fallen over the years was because, over time, the neurotypicals fell by the wayside. Now I can only speak for my own Autistic experience, but what I have established about my own neurotypical ex-friends is that an undercurrent, or visible current, of jealousy developed, and this is part of the reason those friendships no longer exist or were easier to end (even if the primary reason for ending the friendship was something else entirely). Jealousy was part of the demise. At first, people love us – our masks can be very alluring, people are drawn to us for the enigma that we appear – but, in reality, it is the mask they love, and over time they can learn to hate what is underneath. They take the privilege of seeing behind the mask, privilege that we have afforded them through our over trust, and sometimes use what they see against us, to the extent that some will use our own self-deprecating words back at us as theirs. They may deny it to themselves, and to others, but it exists, and jealousy is a poison that slowly damages relationships. I've seen evidence in words, subtle comments that did not go unmissed and behaviours. My greatest vulnerability in authoring this book is that others from my past may choose to use the content in a negative way, to address their pain and to reignite mine. Fortunately, my quest to find lost people far outweighs that fear.

Like many females with Autism, I am vulnerable, and I am also a perfectionist. I remember when I worked in the voluntary sector, the team I worked with nicknamed me 'our perfect being', which revealed itself from the mouths of drunken colleagues at a Christmas party: "This is Jane, she is our 'perfect' being," as I was introduced to their husbands. I felt uncomfortable by it because I knew perfectionism was in no way healthy, or indeed a real compliment, and it revealed to me that if others could see it then the negative trait must exist within me. If you are around a perfectionist, and are taken in by their veneer of perfectionism, that too can make you feel inferior. Any negative internalisation of someone else's accolade or perfectionism is a breeding ground for jealousy, whether that jealousy is conscious, or otherwise. Instead of sharing the joy of someone's achievement, doubling the pleasure for all concerned, it becomes a source of destruction.

Some Allistics come to recognise that they no more fit in with us, or are like us, than we already know about our fitting in with them. It's a newer experience for them, though. Not fitting in is familiar for us, it is the story of our lives! Some will seek the Au-some, the enigma, then realise they cannot mirror it, they are not like us. But they rarely seek the Autistic. They show us their aversion to Autism by their rejection of us when we reveal a little of what is behind the mask. They want our Au-some but not our difference. Autistic people are rainbows, a spectrum of colour, which runs from vibrant to dark, the yin and the yang. Both are one, and cannot be separated, you cannot have one without the other.

I am unable to change my brain, I need external motivators that a neurotypical may not, I need predictability. I am not trying to make others feel less, because no one is inferior or superior to another. But in my pattern-spotting mind, the neurotypicals fell away from my life because a person with lower self-esteem cannot sustain being around me, they learn to hate everything I am. The reason my friend Sam remains a lifelong neurotypical friend is quite simply the fact that she has enough self-esteem and self-worth for us both put together! Everything I am does not reduce her, she feels good about herself and her life, and anything in it that is not as she would like, she takes responsibility and changes that. She has an internal Locus of Control[33]. Off the back of the Covid pandemic, my friend Sam took a life-changing career decision to leave a very long-term job where she was well-thought, a job many would only ever dream of. She too is on a new journey of self-discovery, a journey we will no doubt share together.

I think it is fair to say that one of my obsessions has to be self-obsession. I don't like that; I don't want to be self-indulgent or self-obsessed, but I am enormously more self-

WHAT THEY DON'T PREPARE YOU FOR

aware than most people. This is borne of a lifetime of not knowing, searching for who I am, and trying to navigate a world that is socially complex for an Autistic person. It is also illustration that everything in life has to start with us; it cannot start with others first. We have to look inward to understand the outward. It's also the very case for self-care not being an act of selfishness but an act of necessity if we are to survive and if we are to help others. You simply cannot do that if you do not protect and save yourself first.

Another recognisable pattern I have identified is I can divide my past and present Autistic and Allistic friends by one factor – all my Autistic (diagnosed or undiagnosed) friends have at least one divorce or significant relationship breakdown behind them. My past and present Allistic friends do not. My experience may not be representative of the masses of Autistic people, and I am always conscious of bias in my thinking, in particular 'availability heuristic bias'[34], overestimating and leaping too far with my thinking through information easiest to retrieve, or most salient. There is only one true way of establishing the reliability and validity of such patterns and that is to conduct empirical research, not anecdotal. That said, given my Autistic superpower is pattern-spotting, I would likely have a higher statistical probability of being correct than someone without that natural ability. My husband has always complained that I have to analyse *everything*! I would argue, as Simon Baron-Cohen does in his latest book *The Pattern Seekers*[35], that I have a systemising brain present in many Autistics and inventors, and my specialist area is systemising human behaviour. I take what is unpredictable and seek patterns to understand what I can otherwise not. I use my scientific findings to understand social interactions, predict human behaviour, and to circumvent my greatest fear – conflict. My pattern-seeking human prediction also benefits my business in so many ways. The number of times I say to my associate trainer Gemma, "Trust me, I can see it coming." Gemma understands me, and today recognises I'm not actually trying to fortune tell.

My neuroscope and obsessive-thinking did not stop at my friendship group, or family members, whom I have question-marked because of patterns there too. It also extends to people attending my training courses. Of course, I cannot say or do anything, and I do not, but my neuroscope has them in plain sight. There have been several people since my diagnosis in June, and there are two I have spotted in the films we use in some of the courses I deliver. I do not believe any of them know they could be autistic. I also do not know if any of them would benefit from that knowledge, and it is most certainly not my place to tell them what I think. However, because of the nature of my work, I do share my own lived experience of misdiagnosed anxiety disorders and later Autism diagnosis. When it's relevant, I share snippets of the things I highlight in my book. I have delivered many training courses since my diagnosis in June, including some lived experience talks. In December, the first few people with whom I had shared my story, and who connected with it, came back to tell me they too had now been formally diagnosed Autistic. I predicted this would happen. It has taken five months for the first few people to connect with my experience, self-identify, and to be clinically diagnosed. I recognise the first few to be the private assessments, which can be turned around more quickly, and I anticipate the NHS ones to come in the next twelve to twenty-four months. Each one finds a place in my thoughts and a place in my heart, and *nothing* makes me happier than knowing someone has been found and their suffering has been reduced. It also highlights that stories and narrative have the power to change lives!

My neuroscope does not have an off button, so it does not stop there, it also extends to celebrities and people in the public limelight, past and present…

The Chapter That Wasn't;
The Edit That Became

During the Summer of 2021, not long after my own diagnosis, I became fixated and obsessed with a very well-known successful celebrity. I had always been a fan, but during this time I had seen some footage of the person that revealed to me a likelihood that they could be Autistic. From this identification, I sought to read as much biography about that person as I could. Very early into the reading, I was near certain that this person had an autistic profile.

This celebrity is deceased, and legally it is permissible to write about someone who has passed away with little risk of litigation (though there are, of course, some legal technicalities). You may be thinking… but is it even respectful to pseudo-pathologise someone, let alone someone who is no longer alive?! And yes, I worry greatly about how disrespectful it may be for me to write even this much.

The point for me was that this celebrity's story could help others, and I felt it was possible to do so, and do so respectfully, by seeking the blessing of the person's family in their own absence. From reading about this person, I also felt they would *want* to help others. Everything I had read suggested they were a person of empathy and kindness. So, I wrote to the person's family requesting their permission, and made my case for why I felt it was of public interest. You are reading this edit today because that permission was not granted. It was not granted by way of omission – no response to my draft manuscript or cover letter was ever received.

I made three polite attempts at contact, with a number of family members, and stated my case to each. I wanted to include this person in my book because I thought their story was of public interest for four specific reasons. I will not cite these reasons as it will likely reveal who that person is, which I'm attempting to avoid. Suffice to say, I will highlight one reason, and that reason was that many lost people will connect with this person's story, where they may not connect with my own. The celebrity's story could have led them to self-identification. It could have found them. This celebrity was very different to me, famous for one, yet similar in so many other ways. I felt a personal connection with them, even beyond obsession. Very sadly, this person died young, and in my personal opinion, their (potential) undiagnosed autism contributed to their premature death. This person's life is more than reason enough to find other lost people. Lost people are dying, and that is not me being overly dramatic, it is fact – autism takes years off lives. This person's passing was a huge loss to arts and culture, and undoubtedly to their family.

I have left the door open. I would love to author a book

specifically about this celebrity and to make my theoretical case. I am not the only one to theorise that this celebrity had undiagnosed autism. As part of my research, I came across a journal article that made the case based on the same material that had brought me to my conclusion. It is already in the public domain, though it's not easy to find. I believe it is possible to test our theory. I believe the way to find this celebrity is to find those around them alive today who are also autistic, those who share the same gene pool, and also those who connected and befriended the person during their lifetime, including celebrity friends still alive today. From my own Autism assessment, I also know that it is possible to reach a pretty solid conclusion about diagnosis even if you have not yet met a person, provided you have the level of biographical detail required for clinical judgement. I believe there is a lot of literature and footage available for a prospective diagnosis, even in this person's absence. The question is: is that a leap too far?

Let's say that my theory *is* correct, and this person (and others) receive a late diagnosis of Autism. If I am correct, then we know that at least one lost person died, very likely because they weren't found sooner and never had their autistic needs met. Very sadly, it is easy to illustrate that this person showed signs of suffering, and we may speculate further to say that, had they known their truth, they might even be here with us today. If I had received my diagnosis even fifteen years earlier, authored this book earlier, managed to get my story to that person, the course of direction could have been so different. That we will never know.

Though finding this person will not bring them back, it is possible to show them not only as the amazing artist they were, but as an Autistic icon of our time, held up there with other famous Autistics like Elon Musk, Bill Gates, Steve Jobs, Anthony Hopkins, Darryl Hannah, Dan Ackroyd, Albert Einstein and Michelangelo (the last two suspected but not diagnosed), the list is long. I believe it is never too late to be found. Very sadly, this person will never experience the emancipation, the validation and the freedom from their chains that self-identification could have provided.

My celebrity obsession is a current person obsession whom I have studied at length. I have not had a 'person obsession' since my teens, so this is unusual, and again something I wasn't prepared for after diagnosis.

On the back of my obsessive focus on the (potential) lost celebrity, I have identified a pattern within the arts more generally. As a new writer, I have started to move in and amongst other writers and authors. I can already see a disproportionately high number of people with autistic traits in the writing community. This would make sense. Autistics have difficulties in social communication, but in many cases little difficulty in communicating through other media. We are writers, musicians and artists because these offer us an alternative safer way to express and communicate, somewhat like the visually impaired person who has an acute sense of hearing that is compensating for the visual deficit. We become proficient in the alternative ways because we find them easier to use, so use them more

207

often. I, for example, will always prefer a text or an email to you calling me. I don't like phone calls. It gives me time to process, plan my response, and to communicate in a way that I feel comfortable. It causes me less anxiety.

As well as my lifelong love of writing, I love to sing, but I have never been able to sing in front of others; for example, at karaoke. Or if I have sung on karaoke, say informally at a family Christmas party, I need to sit with my back to people to sing, I cannot look at anyone. It physically pains me to sing and look at you.

My biggest school social faux pas was to volunteer to do a duet with my best friend Sharon of Whitney Houston's 'How Will I Know?' on stage in front of the whole school! Yes, the contradiction with English class is not lost on me either – can't stand up in front of an English class of twenty kids and sing, instead goes on stage and sings in front of three school year groups of 250 kids! I dreamed big, and I genuinely think my bravery can be commended, since even people without anxiety probably wouldn't attempt this. Was it just sheer stupidity, I ask myself? I did step out of my comfort zone despite the fear. It was a disaster, I could not bring myself to sing, I mimed, and I wanted to die. I bailed out of the second performance the following day and left poor Sharon to do it on her own. It still haunts me today, that and the peeing in front of thirty kids at the age of six. These traumas I am sure contributed to an inability to cope in group situations from there on in. To add insult to injury, I later overheard Mr He-Lust-Rious complimenting the female dance troupe who had done, "Such an amazing performance!" said loud enough to ensure I heard, and to highlight just how bad I was and his disdain for me. The desire to impress him, and others, and not to mess up, meant I so often did. It is also the very reason I put a great deal of preparation into every public speaking performance I do today.

Fortunately, that performance did not quash my love of singing and music. I can sing in front of those I can down-mask with, my daughter, my boys and my husband, but not anyone else. In fact, there is nothing I enjoy more than sitting in an Italian restaurant with my daughter Laura and quietly singing Dean Martin's 'That's Amore' in an Italian accent. She gets so embarrassed, which makes it all the more pleasurable! Even Oliver has worked out it is the height of McNeice family entertainment. It only falls second to when she climbs in the car next to me, riding shotgun, and I say, "Well, lady! Lucky you! You just got yourself a front row ticket to the Jane McNeice show!" before singing my heart out to her while she cringes and begs me to stop. I love singing, but the masked Jane cannot sing (or dance) in front of those she masks amongst, only the unmasked version can, so I generally sing and dance when alone. That said, I managed to down-mask and genuinely tried to care less at my daughter's wedding to Alex in November 2019. It would, of course, be a one-time only exhibition that few would witness. I literally had to psychologically detach myself from my surroundings and the other guests to do it. It was my daughter's special day and I really wanted to enjoy it. I switched off my social inhibitions and tried just to be. I danced, and it made me happy!

On reflection, my being prepared for diagnosis looked like this. I knew I was going on a journey, not quite sure where, I'd just been told to pack an overnight bag. So, I'd loaded my bag with PJs, a sundress, towel, beachwear, flip-flops and sunscreen. My journey turned out to be a hiking one! I needed a rucksack, walking boots, crampons and a warm jacket. I wasn't even nearly fit for purpose. Fortunately, I had the right people join me in that journey. They gave me a jacket, warm socks, hat and gloves, refreshments and passed me the goggles and blister cream for when it got tough. I am grateful to those who have supported me.

CHAPTER ELEVEN

Who or What Saves Me Now?

"The most powerful weapon on earth is the human soul on fire."[36]

Ferdinand Foch

Not everyone who is diagnosed Autistic finds it life changing. I did. And some who have been diagnosed Autistic say, "Nothing has changed, it's not like I'm now getting more support." At present, our family has only recently started to receive support in a more tangible way; we now have a Family Support Worker who is supporting us to parent our (yet undiagnosed) autistic son, my older diagnosed Autistic daughter, myself, and our other son Ben, who inevitably finds himself in the position of young carer at times.

Direct support is starting to materialise but change in society is much slower. I have worked hard to survive as an undiagnosed autistic person up to the age of forty-five, and I have always placed the responsibility for my survival solely on me. On the back of my diagnosis, I have displaced that a little, and now believe there are others in society who have a responsibility to help me too – my GP, social services, the government, and others supporting vulnerable people, especially when they are at their *most* vulnerable. Nevertheless, I still take most of the responsibility for my survival.

Another automatic change on the back of my diagnosis is that I now have a greater desire *to* survive. I want to live because I see a much brighter future ahead. My life has gone from black and white to technicolour! I am realistically optimistic, I am not talking eutopia, it doesn't exist. I know there will be ups and downs, but not the downs and the dark side I have experienced in the past. I now have an explanation for the dark side, which helps. I knew getting a diagnosis would not physically change anything on the outside, it never needed to, because it changed the things that mattered most, the inside. The only part we really *can* change. The diagnosis became an intervention in and of itself. The diagnosis saved me.

Having said that, I recognise there are times I can be highly vulnerable, and because of this I have a suicide safety plan in place. Yes, I have one, and anyone who has suicidal thoughts should have one. There is a great phone application called 'Stay Alive'[37] produced by an incredible suicide prevention organisation called Grassroots; you can keep the plan on your phone, to be used at times when it feels like the pain is exceeding the resources for coping with pain. Sadly, that is when a suicide takes place. Ideas around selfishness or lack of selfishness are not the reasons I am alive today. The reason I am alive today is because someone listened to my pain and reduced it. There is no magic formula, other than compassion and empathy. In my head, I have worked out a written formula for suicide, or not to suicide, and I am sure that someone like my ex-father-in-law who has a superior maths ability could apply numbers to this, as my skill extends only to the theory itself:

+/- pain (always layered with loss) + +/- resources = suicide (or not)

To prevent a suicide taking place, we need to do one of two things, but ideally both – reduce someone's pain and/or increase their resources for coping with it – and when this happens, we shift the outcome from being: I want to die, to instead one of: I am going to choose life over death, I want to live. If you are supporting a person with suicidal thoughts, reducing their pain by something as simple as effective listening with understanding and compassion can be enough, but if we can be the holder of hope as well, help the person to feel things can and will get better, then the person may choose life as the preferred option. I always held a belief that life could get better, that there was an answer to be found. Maybe that is why I have survived through the painful times. Through the training that my company offers, we teach people to perform suicide interventions based on these and other principles. I believe my job is one of the most rewarding jobs in the world; at its best it saves lives! I'm pretty sure it has also saved my own.

My diagnosis did for me two significant things, it

reduced the pain and the darkness, and whilst I lost the hope that there would ever be an effective intervention for my ever-present anxiety, I gained resources by now knowing who I am. My risk of suicide is lower than it was pre-diagnosis, and when I have suicidal thoughts, they are mostly passive not active. But I still have a safety plan. I have a safety plan today, not because my psychiatrist told me to in 2019, but because I want to live, and I have a future ahead of me I now want to be part of. I feel alive for the first time ever, and I want to stay that way. There are too many things I want to do, too many people I want to help, and I cannot do that if I am not here. I know my life's purpose.

As an Autistic person, I am statistically likely to have suicidal thoughts more than a neurotypical, several times more likely in fact. Statistical risk does not mean I *will* die by suicide, it just means there is a greater risk that I might. I do not want to become a statistic, and I do not want to cause a pain for my family that could put them at risk too. So, because of this, rather than any medical instruction, I now have a safety plan, of which you are already aware. It is basic, but I know when I am at greatest risk and who I will call upon at that time. There are people in my everyday world who are part of my safety plan. They know who they are, though I in no way pass the responsibility for my survival on to them. Only I am truly responsible for my survival, which is why I did not stop searching for my truth for the last forty-five years. No one should carry the burden of someone else's life, or loss of life, on their shoulders. I believe suicide prevention is a collective societal responsibility, just like the one we all share in protecting one another from Covid-19.

It very much feels like life is coming at me fast at the moment; it feels like the universe is returning to me the last forty-five years in one year. In August this year, I was asked to set five goals as part of a trauma training course I attended. The goals I set were:

1. Run the London Marathon 3rd October – DONE
2. Write my memoir by 2025 – DONE
3. Find the answers to unanswered questions about Autism through a master's degree or PhD – CURRENTLY EXPLORING
4. Deliver positive change and awareness through speaking my truth via my networks – ONGOING
5. Find my son's truth; and help to find the truth for my grandchildren – 2nd December (hopefully!) and beyond…
6. Not being one to avoid going the extra mile, I set an overall goal: PRIORITISE TAKING CARE OF ME (ALWAYS) – VERY ACTIVE AND ONGOING

Prior to my diagnosis, I had a desire to write down my experience; I even started a loose draft, but filed it under B1N (rubbish bin) and started again post-diagnosis. A part of me knew there was a therapeutic benefit in journaling and writing down how I felt. Writing is a great medium for someone who cannot express how they feel verbally.

Writing my life down on paper (okay, laptop) has helped with all the reprocessing that has needed to happen, and has helped to purge some of the internalised thoughts and feelings that had been buried. I had always wanted to author a book, it was one of my many dreams, but I had no real story to write, and simply authoring a book without one would have seemed far too self-indulgent and unjustified. I now know my book was not yet previously meant to happen. When the story unfolded, so too would the book, but my journey was not yet complete. This was the real reason it could not be written; the universe had not yet finished its plan – my story had no ending.

I do believe everyone has a story, even those who do not believe they do. Stories and narrative have shaped our history and culture for time, and everyone has one, though not all will share theirs. It takes bravery because it is an exceptionally vulnerable thing to do. At the start of my writing, I did not appreciate just how vulnerable it would make me feel. In my experience, however, it takes more courage to speak my story than to write it, as you might expect in an Autistic person. Speaking it is like stripping naked in front of your audience, not impossible, but incredibly uncomfortable and exposing.

Since my diagnosis, some people have said, "You do not need to be defined by your Autism." On the contrary, yes, I do. I would not want to be defined by Autism if it were an illness or a disease; I do not define myself by my anxieties, for example. But Autism is not an illness, it is a condition, and it is my identity, an identity I have waited a lifetime

216

to find. In fact, I consider my Autism my most *important* identity, more so than the fact that I am female, a wife, or even a mum. This is why I use identity-first language to describe it. I do not consider my other identities of less value, but how my brain is wired dictates and contributes to all those other identities. My Autistic brain shapes how they are understood, interpreted, communicated and presented, ergo Autism is the nucleus of who I am. This is me. I am Autistic, and I am proud.

I have marked my identity recognition and defined myself by having a tattoo – that disclosure is going to shock a few people! It symbolises my neuro-type on my body – and is in no way a midlife crisis, I might add. In indelible form, the words 'I stopped searching the day I found Au-some' with a small umbrella at the start, marking the start and end to my search. The body art goes all the way around my torso, around my core. My tattoo represents the birth of a woman who is no longer lost, and from the little umbrella and words on my lower back flows a delicate and colourful floral belt towards my front, representing a brighter way forward, a future I am looking forward to for the first time ever. I am creative and have always loved art, but I have never had any desire for body art. As it turns out, it was more the case that I had never found anything so meaningful that I would want to permanently inscribe it into my skin, but like my Autism, it is now me. And I love it!

I have for a long time believed my life's purpose was to reduce mental health suffering. I had committed my career and whole self to it, and it is without doubt a contributory to my life's purpose. It is linked. Today I *know* that my true life's purpose is to find those who are lost, and who, by finding their truth, will in many cases reduce their own suffering. My greatest concern is for those who are searching and in mental pain. I am not intentionally looking for those who are not. I have a fire in my belly that cannot and will not be extinguished; it is driving me to be someone I have not in the past been, an activist, both for myself and for my people.

I am fully aware of the people in both my past *and* present who are autistic. Some of them know or are close to knowing themselves, some of them have no idea whatsoever, and some of them could not care less. Of those who are interested, some of them would like a diagnosis, and some of them would not. That is their right and certainly not mine. In some cases, I did not identify those people because I have witnessed their suffering, but because I have witnessed their autistic traits, which, on reflection, were or are quite obvious. They are obvious because they are themselves, their true autistic selves. I admire this.

The pattern I identify in the suffering, or not suffering, appears to come down to how much, or how little, an autistic person socially masks. The social masking comes down to how much an autistic person feels they don't fit in plus how much they want to, and the level of searching I believe comes down to how much both are present, plus the person's IQ. But I'd like to test that theory scientifically. I would like to find those individuals, which in many cases will be women, who, like I was, are living a life lost and suffering. That purpose will be a huge part of what helps me now.

> *"The curious paradox is that when I accept myself just as I am, then I can change."*[38]
>
> Carl Rogers

Carl Rogers knew a thing or two about incongruence as it turns out. He knew we needed to be ourselves not to suffer, but what is missing in the above Rogerian quote is that 'to *accept* ourselves we first need to know who and what we are, what it *is* that we are accepting'. Now that I know who I am, I can work on what I would like to change.

I know my masks are suffocating me, and have been doing so for a long time, they do need to be removed. Until I can learn to do that, I will continue to need lots of alone time to offset their impact. I now *recognise* that need, accommodate it, and do so without apology. My previous fear of loneliness has naturally dissipated, I am no longer scared of rejection. I no longer live by neurotypical ideals to fulfil my worth. I am slightly less scared of people, more likely to speak my truth and recognise that our family is different to others. Because our family is different, there may come a time that we need to live in a unique way to survive. My husband and I have reflected that our home is not the right living environment conducive to the Autistic needs of those living in it, and to our basic needs. For example, I need a place to restore, a place of solitude, but our current home does not offer this. I must attempt to take my head away instead, through reading. This is how I cope on vacations when I am with people 24/7 for a week or more, otherwise I go AWOL for a few hours on my own. Oliver is also learning he needs solitude, especially after a meltdown. Our current home was a house purchased before both boys were born, and we have now outgrown it, especially when we factor the needs that we are today acknowledging. Our home is something we will need to change at the earliest opportunity, and it will likely mean moving house, a change that will be exceptionally difficult for Oliver and me to come to terms with because we both struggle with change. Home will stop being our haven for a few weeks, we will feel out of sorts, but we will adjust, and in time it will become safe and protective again. We must play the long game.

I still have a long way to go, but the natural shift is already transforming. Things are not perfect, but they are better, more survivable. I have stopped apologising for who I am because I no longer need the approval of others that I did previously, and I will not ever become someone's projection of the negative parts of themselves. I will not be anyone's victim. I now know I deserve better.

My life is testimony to a certain level of resilience in the face of adversity, a tenacity to keep looking for truth, and a journey of patience. I will never regret my continued searching. But my life is also evidence that we do not know enough about Autism. Through reading, researching, and hearing other people's narrative, it has become very obvious to me that there are too many unanswered questions. Notwithstanding the continued professional development I do as part of my work within mental health, I had no previous desire beyond my Post Graduate Certificate in Vocational Rehabilitation to go back into academia, but I have very quickly recognised a reignited yearning to. I now want to go back into academics because I want to find the answers to the big questions about Autism. I want to know if I am alone in my experience, or if the anecdotal patterns I recognise are valid. It is not enough for me to put forth my personal opinion. As an Autistic person, I work with facts. There is only one way to put theories to the test and that is to perform empirical research. I finished my Post Graduate Certificate in 2013, so it's now been a little while since I studied at that level, but I have never stopped searching, absorbing and learning. My hope is to blend my obsession with mental health with my new obsession to greater understand Autism. It may be the case that one obsession envelops the other, to the extent that I may even need to step back from my business to pursue the others further. As yet, I do not know what the future will look like, but I am looking forward to finding out.

Epilogue

Through my own learning and illustrations in this book, there are some stark statistics related to Autism and Autistic people. Sad statistics. But I believe those statistics are not, in most cases, inevitable. Rather, they are evidence of a historical lack of support for Autistic people that has existed and still remains today. As a now diagnosed Autistic person, I should feel confident that I will be supported, that external support will be available and accessible, but sadly I and other Autistic people cannot confidently say that. A gaping hole exists in understanding and support.

It is well documented that research is lacking, particularly research around women with Autism, in part because only a few decades ago we did not even think women could *be* Autistic. We have some serious catching up to do!

Prior to drafting my book, I put a question to the online Autistic community: What would you want others to really understand about Autism? Someone kindly shared a quote they had read written by another Autistic person:

"Life is soup; I am a fork!"
(Unknown Autistic with a unique mind)

If the fork were you, what would you do to support them? Ask yourself, how would you adapt the liquid so the fork could be effective? Should the fork need to adapt? Should we change its environment, move it towards a food where it can be most effective? What should we do?

This lack of understanding and support has an impact on our workplaces, the economy, society, families and individuals. I would personally like to be the change I would like to see in society in respect of Autism, and I have learned that my own neurotypical masking has a negative impact not just on me but other Autistic people too. I am to them what neurotypicals often are to me, lacking in support. "If you think you are too small to make a difference, try sleeping with a mosquito," said the Dalai Lama[39]. What can appear to be insignificant can add up to momentous change.

As an Autistic person, I have a role and responsibility to my tribe. Like others, I too need to hear autistic people in whatever way they communicate, whether communicated through the spoken or written word. Using our ears alone will not be enough, and it is even the case that not everyone in the world has that privilege. Those who have it often listen but fail to hear. We need to use all our senses to hear, we need to use our eyes to observe, our hearts to feel, and to do so with an open mind. Only then can we help in the best way for any Autistic person. I have a responsibility to listen to other Autistic people, to hear their stories, and to use the vehicle and privilege that is my business to channel those stories towards a greater level of understanding and support. Better still, let us all create an Autism revolution! Is it not possible to create a world that is autism friendly regardless of who is, or who isn't, to meet need rather than majority?

Prior to my starting this book, a new piece of research had been launched, an Autism genetics study. There was a prompt and vociferous backlash from the Autistic community, questioning the risks around sharing and usage of genetic data, amongst other concerns. The community launched the campaign 'Boycott Spectrum 10k' on well-known social media platforms, an endeavour to voice itself and assert the power of the community. The research has since been put on hold, for further conversations to take place with the Autistic community. My personal concern is that such research could mean we reignite historical ideas of 'curing' Autism, both from autistic individuals, and from society. To do so could be a disaster for diversity, and an even greater disaster for humanity.

Research illustrates that Autistic people have existed since the dawn of time[40]; nature knew we were needed, otherwise we would have been eradicated through natural selection. That has not happened. On the contrary, many people are now beginning to recognise that if humanity is to find solutions to its 'BIG' problems, for example climate change, then we in fact *need* the minds of Autistic people, as they are likely to address problems in a unique and different way, since the ways that have been used to date are not proving effective. We need the Greta Thunbergs of this world and other revolutionary minds.

Autistic people are different, not less, but rather equals in a human race that needs us, one that we need in return. If we are to belong, we need to be understood, accepted, and supported for who we are, not forced to change. We do not need to be cured, and we do want to be accepted if acceptance is based solely on our ability to adapt, change, or to mirror neurotypical. We need to be our whole Autistic selves without apology. Please don't change us, tune into us. This leaves me just one more thing to say: My name is Jane McNeice, and I am AUTISTIC.

★★★

… and when you thought you had heard my last, today on the 11th of December 2021, I am adding the final jigsaw piece to our story, to our picture: on the 2nd of December, my second child Oliver was officially diagnosed Autistic. His name is Oliver McNeice, and he too is AUTISTIC. He is found, and his story is just beginning…

A Message to My Younger Self

Sweetheart, I know you are troubled, and I know it is painful. You are different, but you are different 'good' not different 'bad.' Hear me now, and hear me loud and clear, your thinking is wrong, and it is flawed, you are simply *different* not wrong. And I am sorry, but it may always feel that way. But please don't die, don't give up, there's a plan for you, all this is the plan. We need it to create the energy and momentum for finding your truth later; there is purpose tomorrow for your pain today. Your journey will deliver your life's purpose. You will heal your own pain, and you will heal others' pain. Please don't leave us yet, don't give up, you have too much to offer the world. But don't forget yourself while trying to help others, your suffering matters, and you are going to need to remember that, always. This pain you feel right now is not in vain. It gets better, I promise you. You don't know me, but I need you to trust me.

PS… and stop wasting money on acne creams, they are not working, time will heal all things, including the acne!

Acknowledgements

There are people past and present to whom I owe my thanks every single day, to some my entire survival. I would like to thank my parents, one of whom is herself trying to survive while lost, and raised two children with Autism – one diagnosed young, and one who would not be diagnosed until later in life. I hope this book illustrates what my parents achieved despite all the challenges, challenges that Mum still faces today. Mum, Dad, I love you both. Thank you also to my mother-in-law Arlene, the only person to ask if she could read my assessment report because she wanted to understand me better.

Whilst he is sadly no longer with us, I would like to thank my late brother for reminding me every day what is possible in the face of adversity, and for bringing a sparkle into my world for forty-one years. That sparkle made my own and other people's world a better one.

Three professionals have played a huge part in my journey over the last eighteen months, they have helped me to find me, supported me to find me, and they have listened to me every step of the way. Thank you to Sarah Brown 'Ideas Inspirer' and she is! To Wendy Crowther, and to Deborah Cullinan. These acknowledgements would in no way be justified if I do not also give thanks to the lovely Clare Parkin who provided counselling to me following the death of my brother and who supported me through some challenging life changes. Your help was never forgotten, though I did forget your name and I apologise for that. Thanks to modern technology I re-found you, and your name!

Thank you to my best girlfriends, Sam, Donna, Vicky, Pam, Karen and my young friend and surrogate daughter Gemma.

I thank Richard McCann at the iCan Academy and his Influence Story Telling Retreat for helping me to public speak my narrative. I thank Cassandra Farren, my writing mentor, who has helped me to document my heart-led story, who has supported me with advice, guidance, motivation, meditation, and reminded me (several times!) that I have a story, someone needs to hear it (right now!), and I should write it (today!). Richard, Cassandra, "I can, I will, I did!" Thank you.

Thank you to Jen Parker, my editor, who applied her pink flamingo and some sparkle to the final draft. I don't know what you did, but you made it sparkle! Thank you to Collette Evans at Picture Perfect Photography for her photographic skills and creativity, and showing me in my best light, despite my dislike of personal photographs! And thank you to Craig Richardson at Combine Studio for whipping this up into a great website for my book!

Thank you to Karl Matthews at Blood Brothers for my tattoo, and his mum who makes *the* best cinder toffee ever!

Lastly, and by no means lesser in measure, thank you to my husband Steven, who started as fun, became my soulmate, and still throws in a dash of fun! Thank you to my first born, my daughter Laura, who listens to me daily, indulges my mind, my ideas, and 'gets it' where very few others do. Thank you to my boys, Ben who shows me what it is like to be neurotypical in a neurotypical world, and Oliver who teaches me every day that love and compassion are the true answers to everything. Thank you to my wonderful grandchildren. Becoming a grandma at a young age means we all get to spend even more time in one another's lives, it is a privilege.

There are also people who, without their intervention and ripple effect, the last two years would not have taken the direction it has, Oliver for being himself, and by doing so opening our eyes to difference, my husband for questioning and instigating the search and our subsequent finds. Thank you to Arabel who recommended I take a look at Sunshine CIC on Facebook, the support page for parents of children with Autism, without which I would not have found me. Thank you to Sunshine Support CIC for putting awareness out there for me to find, and thank you to the online Autistic community who tirelessly offer their empathy and support to others while trying to survive themselves. I owe all of you an eternal debt for giving me a future different to my past.

And finally... Thank you to Mrs Wall from the wool shop in Thorne, for allowing me to pick up the little umbrellas every Saturday afternoon and allowing me to declutter her shop floor. I hope it made her feel as comforted as it did me.

About the Author

Jane McNeice lives in South Yorkshire with her husband, two boys, her cat Angel, and a 7-month-old cocker spaniel called Chester who was recently bestowed upon her, and whom she is slowly learning to love.

Jane is Director of Mind Matters, and when she is not spending time with her family, reading, or enjoying a nice cuppa, she can be found searching for 'Lost Girls' and raising awareness of Autism, or delivering mental health training. Jane enjoys running and audiobooks as part of looking after her own mental health and considers herself very much a 'work in progress' inside and out, but aren't we all...

References

Note: Where the work of others has been referenced, the Author has made every effort to ensure that the source is identified through appropriate citation. If you believe a piece of work has been omitted, or has been cited incorrectly, the Author will be pleased to make the appropriate acknowledgements or revisions in any future edition.

1. *'Unknown Wise Man'* in Silberman, Steve (2015), *NeuroTribes: The Legacy of Autism and How to Think Smarter About People Who Think Differently*, Publisher: Allen & Unwin

2. Roman-Urrestarazu, R et al. *Association of Race/Ethnicity and Social Disadvantage with Autism Prevalence in 7 Million School Children in England*. JAMA Paediatrics; 29 March 2021; DOI: 10.1001/jamapediatrics.2021.0054

3. American Psychiatric Association. (2013). Anxiety disorders. In *Diagnostic and statistical manual of mental disorders* (5th ed.). https://doi.org/10.1176/appi. books.9780890425596.dsm05 [online]

4. Dr Lorna Wing, pioneer in the field of childhood developmental disorders, describes Autistic difficulties as, "Social, social, social, it's *all* social." 3rd May 2011

National Autistic Society 'Interview with Dr Lorna Wing' https://www.youtube.com/watch?v=L_4loBEg9kw [online]

5. Kanner, L. Autistic disturbances of affective contact. *Nervous Child* **2**, 217-250 (1943)

6. Autistica (2021) https://www.autistica.org.uk/what-is-autism/signs-and-symptoms/learning-disability-and-autism [online]

7. Higashida, N. (2013) *The Reason I Jump: the inner voice of a thirteen-year-old boy with autism.* First edition. New York: Random House.

8. Baio J, Wiggins L, Christensen DL, et al. Prevalence of Autism Spectrum Disorder Among Children Aged 8 Years – Autism and Developmental Disabilities Monitoring Network, 11 Sites, United States, 2014. MMWR Surveill Summ 2018; 67 (No. SS-6): 1-23 DOI: https://www.cdc.gov/mmwr/volumes/67/ss/ss6706a1.htm?s_cid=ss6706a1_w [online]

9. 28th March 2018 – Channel Four documentary 'Are you Autistic' https://www.channel4.com/programmes/are-you-autistic

10. Autism Act 2009 https://www.legislation.gov.uk/ukpga/2009/15/contents [online]

11. Interview with Dr Stephen Shore: Autism Advocate & on the Spectrum, on Lime Network https://www.limeconnect.com/opportunities_news/detail/leading-perspectives-on-disability-a-qa-with-dr-stephen-shore [online]

12. Maslow's Hierarchy of Needs – Wikipeidia 2021

https://en.wikipedia.org/wiki/Maslow%27s_hierarchy_of_needs [online]

13. Mandy, W., Chilvers, R., Chowdhury, U., Salter, G., Seigal, A., & Skuse, D. (2012). *Sex differences in autism spectrum disorder: evidence from a large sample of children and adolescents*. J Autism Dev Disorder, 42 (7), 1304-1313.

14. Meredith Goldberg Edelson (2010) *Sexual Abuse of Children with Autism: Factors that Increase Risk and Interfere with Recognition of Abuse*, Disability Studies Quarterly https://dsq-sds.org/article/view/1058/1228 [online]

15. The Myers Briggs Foundation (2021) MBTI https://www.myersbriggs.org/my-mbti-personality-type/mbti-basics/ [online]

16. Belbin Team Roles Inventory https://www.belbin.com/about/belbin-team-roles [online]

17. Neil Fleming – VARK guide to learning preferences https://vark-learn.com/introduction-to-vark/the-vark-modalities/ [online]

18. Honey & Mumford – learning styles https://www.eln.co.uk/blog/honey-and-mumford-learning-styles [online]

19. Baron-Cohen, S. (1995). *Mindblindness: An essay on autism and theory of mind.* The MIT Press.

20. The National Autistic Society 'The Double Empathy Problem' https://www.autism.org.uk/advice-and-guidance/professional-practice/double-empathy [online]

21. Kroenke, K., Spitzer, R.L. Williams, J.B., *et al.* (2007) *Anxiety disorders in primary care: prevalence, impairment,*

comorbidity, and detection. Annals of Internal Medicine **146**(5), 317-325.

22. Suicide & Autism (Autistica) https://www.autistica.org.uk/what-is-autism/signs-and-symptoms/suicide-and-autism [online]

23. Hull, L., Petrides, K.V. & Mandy, W. *The Female Autism Phenotype and Camouflaging: a Narrative Review*. *Rev J Autism Dev Disorder* **7**, 306–317 (2020). https://doi.org/10.1007/s40489-020-00197-9 [online]

24. Sunshine Support CIC [online] https://www.sunshine-support.org/ [online]

25. Friedrich Nietzsche (1844-1900) *The Gay Science Book IV* – Aphorism #290

26. Cassidy, S., Bradley, L., Shaw, R. et al. Risk markers for suicidality in autistic adults. *Molecular Autism* **9,** 42 (2018). https://doi.org/10.1186/s13229-018-0226-4 [online]

27. Arthur Schopenhauer, German philosopher (1788 – 1860)

28. Joel Whitton (1986) *Life between Life: Scientific Explorations into the Void Separating One Incarnation from the Next*, Publisher: Harper Collins Distribution Centre

29. Weiss, Brian (2004) *Same Soul, Many Bodies*, Publisher: Piatkus

30. Ntara, Caroline (2003-2022) Labelling Theory, Study.com https://study.com/learn/lesson/labeling-theory.html [online]

31. Kubler-Ross, D., & Kessler, E. (2014). *On Grief and Grieving*. Simon & Schuster.

32. Karla Fisher (2012) *Autistic Grief is not like Neurotypical*

Grief http://www.thinkingautismguide.com/2012/08/autistic-grief-is-not-like-neurotypical.html [online]

33. Gabriel Lopez-Gorrido (2020) Locus of Control, Simply Psychology https://www.simplypsychology.org/locus-of-control.html [online]

34. Waters, Shonna Phd (2021) The Cognitive Biases Caused by the Availability Heuristic, BetterUp https://www.betterup.com/blog/the-availability-heuristic [online]

35. Baron-Cohen, Simon (2020) *The Pattern Seekers: How Autism drives human invention*, Publisher: Basic Books

36. Ferdinand Foch (1851-1929) – French military commander during WW1.

37. Grassroots 'Stay Alive App' https://www.prevent-suicide.org.uk/find-help-now/stay-alive-app/ [online]

38. Rogers, Carl (1995) *On Becoming a Person: A Therapist's View of Psychotherapy*, Publisher: Houghton Mifflin (Trade)

39. Goodreads (2022) https://www.goodreads.com/quotes/7777-if-you-think-you-are-too-small-to-make-a [online]

40. Rudacille, Deborah (2011) Lonely Hunters, Spectrum https://www.spectrumnews.org/opinion/lonely-hunters/ [online]

Contact Jane

If after reading my book you learn that you too are a 'Lost Girl' and would like to share your story, please contact me. The 'Lost Girls' need to have their voices heard, and my intention is to bring together a collaboration of all our stories through future published works.

Email: hello@umbrellapicker.co.uk

www.umbrellapicker.co.uk

www.mindmatterstraining.co.uk

LinkedIn: Jane McNeice

Made in the USA
Las Vegas, NV
19 November 2022

59803435R00138